EARTH PILGRIM

EARTH
PILGRIM

SATISH KUMAR

in conversation with

Echan Deravy and Maya Kumar Mitchell

with drawings by Cecil Collins

green books

Published in 2009
by Green Books Ltd
Foxhole, Dartington, Totnes, Devon TQ9 6EB
edit@greenbooks.co.uk www.greenbooks.co.uk

Drawings by Cecil Collins (1909–1989)
© Tate, London 2009:

Frontispiece: The Pilgrim (1944)
page 8: Fool and flower (1944)
page 14: Fool and flowers (1944)
page 34: A Fool praying (1976)
page 52: Head (1974)
page 88: Fool (1976)
page 100: Tree and hills (1944)
page 118: Head (1944)

Cover design by Stephen Prior

Text printed by The Cromwell Press Group, Wiltshire, UK
on Five Seasons Book-White 100% recycled paper

ISBN 978 1 900322 57 7

CONTENTS

ACKNOWLEDGEMENTS

One day in spring 2008, Echan Deravy, a Scotsman living in Japan, came to Hartland in north Devon, where my wife June and I live and where we also have the offices of *Resurgence* magazine. Echan had been working on a project making films and books under the title of 'Earth Pilgrims'. I too had made a film with the same title, which was screened on BBC2 during the winter of 2008. When Echan heard about the film he was delighted, and he approached me and asked me if I would spend two or three days with him, talking about the meaning of pilgrimage, for a film he was making. Out of those conversations a manuscript emerged. So really it is thanks to Echan that the idea of writing a book about being a pilgrim came about. But many of the stories of my life that he asked me to narrate are already published in my other books, so much of this material wasn't appropriate for a new book. However, those conversations provided me with a warp on which to start weaving.

I gave Echan's text to my daughter Maya, and we decided to work on it together. Since Maya lives in Barcelona, we had to wait until we both had a week free to work on the book. At the beginning of February 2009 Maya finally came to Devon, and we were able to avail ourselves of the hospitality of Claire and Roger Ash-Wheeler, in their beautiful cottage on the Cornish coast. There, close to the crashing white waves of the Atlantic, Maya and I discussed and grappled with more ideas, and found ourselves exploring new horizons. During this time the writing grew into a series of questions and reflections about the nature of pilgrimage, and the spirit of the pilgrim.

This first draft I gave to my wife June. Over the years June and I have talked and talked about all matters related to spirituality, philosophy, Jain and Buddhist thinking, and recollected many Hindu stories. June has been my source of inspiration, and we have travelled together as pilgrims. Everything I have written has unfolded from the life we share, so as well as being my editor, she has also been a fellow explorer who has enriched and contributed to all my writings. This book is no exception.

So my thanks go to Echan for initiating this project and carefully transcribing the original conversation. Then my thanks go to Maya for helping me to develop the text and ideas into a book. Special thanks go to June, who worked on the text and fine-tuned it into a more polished script.

Cecil Collins is the artist who best captured the pilgrim spirit in his work, and therefore I am filled with pleasure to be able to incorporate Cecil's drawings in my book. My gratitude goes to Julian Barnard, who has kindly allowed me to reproduce several drawings from his private collection; and to my good friend John Lane, who provided the image used for the Frontispiece. Thanks also to the Tate Gallery, who own the copyright, for their permission to reproduce Cecil's work.

Further thanks and thoughts of gratitude go to Elaine Green and Sophie Poklewski Koziell who have helped this computer-illiterate oldie with the final preparation of this book.

Satish Kumar
Hartland, spring 2009

FOREWORD
by Rupert Sheldrake

Satish Kumar is a visionary who unites his spiritual perspective with a practical concern for bringing human beings together to live better on the Earth and with each other. He has influenced many people through his talks, through his work as Editor of *Resurgence* magazine, which combines ecology and spirituality in a mutually refreshing way, through his work in setting up Schumacher College at Dartington, Devon, as a unique centre for holistic education, and above all by his example. Satish's life is in itself a pilgrimage, as he shows in this book, but this for him is no mere metaphor. After years in India as a wandering monk, his first great international pilgrimage was from India to England via Russia, on foot. In his second great pilgrimage at the age of 50 he walked hundreds of miles between the sacred places of Britain. At 60, he went around the great holy mountain of India and Tibet, Mount Kailash, including travelling through an 18,000-foot-high pass.

His physical pilgrimages remind us of the importance of these Earthly journeys. Here in Britain, as elsewhere in medieval Europe, the land was crisscrossed with the routes of pilgrimages. Geoffrey Chaucer's *Canterbury Tales* are set in the context of England's most popular pilgrimage, and in Catholic Europe pilgrimages still continue to this day, including the journey to Santiago de Compostela at the western gateway of continental Europe on the Galician coast of Spain.

I lived in Satish's home country, India, for seven years. When I arrived, I had been shaped by a secular scientific education, and was quite unprepared for what I found. Among my Indian friends and colleagues, sacred times and places were not vague ideas inherited from the past, but a living part of their lives. Many of my Muslim friends observed the fasts and festivals, and went on pilgrimages to the shrines of Sufi saints, dotted around the countryside near Hyderabad, where I was working in an international agricultural institute. Some aspired to make that great pilgrimage, the Hajj, to Mecca. Hindus went on many sacred journeys, most commonly to Tirupathi, to the shrine of Sri Venkateshwara, a form of the god Vishnu, often coming back with shaven heads and delicious sweets – *prasad* – which had been blessed in the temple, which they shared with me and others so that we too could participate in the blessings their journey had brought. I visited several Hindu temples at the time of festivals, most memorably the shrine of Sri Mookambika, in Kollur, in the hills of Karnataka, where I saw thousands of people who had made long journeys, often on foot, to be present in those holy places at these special times. Their fervour was palpable, but they were also having fun.

When I returned to England from India, I was at first sad to think how much our culture has lost. But then I realised that the sacred places are still there, and so are the great festivals of the Christian tradition. I had been blind to them before. I rediscovered them with gratitude and a new appreciation.

In northern Europe, the Protestant reformers suppressed pilgrimage as a pagan relic. The holy places of Europe were not mentioned in the Bible, naturally enough, since the holy places of the Bible were not those of Europe but of Palestine. The shrine at Canterbury was destroyed, and the image of the Black Madonna of Walsingham, the greatest place of pilgrimage to Our Lady, was burned in a public bonfire. King Henry VIII's troops physically blocked the path of pilgrims. But although the old traditions could be repressed by force, the urge to go on pilgrimage could not, and it was the English who invented its secular substitute, tourism. Tourists still go to sacred places, but do not know what to do when they get there. One of the shifts in attitude which could help us regain a sense of the sacredness of the Earth is to switch back from tourism to pilgrimage. Not only would these journeys become more meaningful, but they would connect with traditions going back through all Christian history to the pre-Christian past, and link to the archetype of sacred journeys found all over the world.

This book is not primarily about Satish's physical pilgrimages, but about their metaphorical extension to life's journey, and indeed to entire evolutionary progress. "A pilgrim is someone who sees life as a sacred journey, who sees the Earth as a sacred home, who sees the universe as a process," as Satish puts it so clearly. The main point of pilgrimage is the inner journey: "We make the outer journey in order to make an inner journey. Our inner landscape is shaped by the outer landscape and vice versa. Therefore, by making a journey to holy places, such as the River Ganges, Mount Kailash, Santiago de Compostela or Iona, we are moved to explore our inner landscape, and make our journey to the holy source within."

This book is fresh, wise, and profound, and is expressed with all Satish's directness and simplicity. It also has the great merit of brevity. Anyone who reads and digests it will find that their life is enriched. Above all, it is inspiring, like Satish himself.

Rupert Sheldrake

INTRODUCTION
Pilgrims or Tourists?

We can relate to our planet Earth in two ways. Either we can act as tourists and look at the Earth as a source of goods and services for our use, pleasure and enjoyment, or we can act as Earth Pilgrims and treat the planet with reverence and gratitude. Tourists value the Earth and all her natural riches only in terms of their usefulness to themselves. Pilgrims perceive the planet as sacred, and recognise the intrinsic value of all life. The living Earth, with all its grace and beauty, is good in itself.

Tourists find gratification in the consumption of nature's gifts. Pilgrims find enchantment in the conservation of nature's bounty. The abundant waters of the oceans, the vibrancy of forests, the community of dancing birds, the tranquillity of valleys and the resilience of magnificent mountains bring a sense of joy, awe and wonder to the hearts of pilgrims. For them, god is nature and nature is their god. Nature is their teacher, their guru and their guide. Sometimes they call her Gaia, the Earth goddess, and at other times they call her simply Mother Nature.

Indigenous people of the world lived and behaved as pilgrims. The Earth was their temple, their church and their mosque. They went into the wild for their vision quest. They sat under the trees for their prayers and meditation, and they did not look up to the sky to find heaven – for their heaven was here on Earth.

St Francis was a pilgrim of this sacred planet. Wolves, birds and all other creatures were his kith and kin; the sun and fire were his brothers; the moon, the stars, the wind and water were his sisters.

For Hindus, god is not a person sitting in paradise. For them, all life is imbibed with the divine. Everything from a blade of grass to the high Himalayas is permeated through and through with the sacred spirit. Hindus consider themselves to be pilgrims on planet Earth.

In all religious traditions there are some special sacred sites: they are like the seven chakras or the acupuncture points of the human body. Pilgrims make journeys to these sites: the holy mounts of Kailash or Athos, the holy rivers of Ganges and Yangtze, and sacred places such as Camino de Santiago de Compostela and the Isle of Iona. It is useful to make outer journeys in order to make inner journeys, but the significant realisation of a pilgrimage is in the consciousness that the whole of the Earth is a sacred site. Of course, every one of us can discover a particular site which resonates with our spirit, where we can go and be in solitude and find ourselves, whether it be a particular tree, or hill, or corner of the seashore. Such special sacred sites can be a significant symbol. In the same way that a mantra is a sound which connects us with the cosmic consciousness, a particular grove, cave or valley can be a point to connect us with the Earth.

The sacred Earth is a gracious host to all pilgrims – but are we prepared to be gracious pilgrim guests, rather than mere tourists?

Normally a book has a beginning, middle and an end, but this book is different because of the circular nature of conversations. Ideas and themes emerge, disappear and return. Through these conversations I am attempting to present a pilgrim's worldview of ethics, aesthetics, spirituality, economics and politics. From a pilgrim's point of view I am on a journey through this world; I see the world as a sacred place and I pass through it with reverence and gratitude, without any desire to possess the world and exploit it for any short-term gain. I hope you enjoy these conversations.

Chapter One

TO BE A PILGRIM

Give me my scallop-shell of quiet,
My staff of faith to walk upon,
My scrip of joy, immortal diet,
My bottle of salvation,
My gown of glory, hope's true gage,
And thus I'll take my pilgrimage.

Sir Walter Raleigh, *The Passionate Man's Pilgrimage*

It's a pleasure and a privilege to be talking with you. I have been following your work through *Resurgence* since the early days. You have gone on pilgrimage many times. Recently I too became a pilgrim, and I found out how difficult it is. To be a pilgrim is to walk the talk. When you're a pilgrim, it's not the physical difficulties you face when you're walking – it's the mental difficulties that arise within you that are so challenging. So the first thing that I'd like to discuss with you is this: what is the difference between ordinary everyday life, and being on a pilgrimage?

For me, there is no difference; life itself is a pilgrimage. To be a pilgrim is to be on the move, physically, mentally and metaphorically. Life is a pilgrimage because life is not static. Life has no ultimate objective. Life is to be lived in every moment. The meaning of life is in the living. As a pilgrim I discover the mystery, the magic, the meaning, the magnificence of life in every step I take, in every sound I hear, in every sight I see.

To be a pilgrim is to experience life as an endless and eternal process of being. Life is not a product, but an ever unfolding process. The moment I think of the word 'pilgrim' I imagine 'movement', 'process', 'unfolding', 'flying' and 'flowing'. To be a pilgrim is just the opposite of being a tourist! As a pilgrim I care less for road-maps and more for the map of the mind. A tourist is travelling to arrive at a place, whereas a pilgrim finds fulfilment in the journey. A pilgrim embraces the unpredictable, the unplanned, the temporary, the ambiguous and the provisional. A pilgrim is an eternal guest.

Guests do not bind themselves to a place, however joyful, comfortable and nice that place may be. The nature of guests is to love and leave. As William Blake said,

He who binds himself a joy
Does the winged life destroy;
But he who kisses the joy as it flies
Lives in eternity's sunrise.

How old were you when you became a pilgrim?

I was four years old.

You started pilgrimages at the age of four?

Yes, because my mother was a pilgrim. She used to take me to her farm, and she would always walk to the farm. She said that "walking to the farm is a pilgrimage," and she said "if we go on horseback or in a camel cart, then we are just interested in getting to the farm. But when we are walking, every step we take is a step of completion, a step of fulfilment, a step towards self-realisation."

You really had a wonderful mother.

Absolutely! She was a truly spiritual being. My mother would say that when you touch the Earth, you are touching a sacred space – a divine space – and god is present in the Earth. And everything upon this Earth is a manifestation of the divine spirit in physical form. Every physical form has an invisible dimension. And that invisible dimension is the divine dimension, the spiritual dimension, the imaginative dimension. You have to imagine that this flower you are looking at is not just a physical flower; it is an embodiment of divine spirit. The flower is an intelligent and animate being.

The way the word imagination is currently used is limited to the idea of artistic imagination, although Thomas Aquinas interpreted imagination in the way you are describing: "It was so that we could actually visualise the invisible."

The physical form is a vehicle to carry the invisible reality. For example, words are a vehicle to carry meaning, to communicate the implicit. Similarly, the body is a vehicle to carry love, carry compassion. When I say to carry love, I also mean to express love, for if you have no body, then how do you embrace somebody? How do you look warmly at somebody? How do you kiss somebody? So, the body is a vehicle to carry that generosity, that love. The body and love can not exist without each other. The flower has a physical form, but it also has an invisible dimension, and that invisible dimension can only be realised through the imagination. In India we have called it the third eye, the eye of the imagination, the eye of the heart. The two eyes are the physical eyes, which can see physical forms; but in order to see non-physical forms you have to have the non-physical third eye, the eye of the spirit. So imagination, from a spiritual point of view, is much bigger than the artistic or poetic imagination. However, the creative imagination is included in the spiritual imagination, because through art and poetry we can reach the divine. For example, William Blake experienced the divine through his paintings and poems, through the "Force of Imagination".

Tagore was another example.

Exactly. Tagore, through his poetry, music, and paintings, was reaching that invisible reality. He was a mystic, and he saw the divine in nature, in people – in fact his songs and poetry give us a glimpse of the divine. This word 'divine' – what do we mean by it? The divine simply means the eternal reality of blissfulness. Eternal and infinite reality is implicit every moment, in everything, in the here and now. The divine is not in the next life. The divine is not in holy books. The divine is not in churches, mosques or temples. The divine is present in every moment and in everything; in every word we speak, in every atom we touch, the divine presence is there. If we don't see the divine in every cell of existence, it is because we lack imagination. We lack a sense of the sacred. We have to imagine that there is a bigger reality in that flower, in that tree, in that river, in that butterfly, in that human being, in that bell, in that sound.

To everything there are two dimensions – the visible dimension and the invisible dimension. The invisible dimension is the divine dimension.

We're talking about two dimensions, but does that not lead to dualism? Are you saying that the visible reality and the invisible reality are separable?

Not at all – they are inseparable. One cannot exist without the other. Spirit and matter are two aspects of one single existence. Without spirit, matter cannot exist. And without matter, spirit cannot exist. So matter needs spirit, and spirit needs matter. Without each other there is no existence. So it's entirely a single, complete, whole. It is called *Purnam* in Sanskrit, meaning a complete and whole reality. But in order to understand the whole, in order to make sense of it in language and with our intellect, sometimes we have to explain it. So this is only a way of analysing and explaining that there is a visible and invisible reality, there is matter and spirit; or, if you like, there is the world and there is god, but they are one and the same and there is no separation.

Does that mean that god (or spirit) comes first, and the world (or matter) is created by god?

Look at it in this way. A room has walls and space. Without the walls there is no room, equally, without the empty space there is no room. So the room is made up of walls and space simultaneously. The Buddhists call it form and emptiness; form is emptiness and emptiness is form. For me, matter represents the form and emptiness represents the spirit. Form is not more primary than emptiness, nor is emptiness primary to form. They are two aspects of the same reality.

Thus, god is not the cause of the world; god is the world. The world was not created by god in six days, and then on the seventh day god went to sleep and the world kept on turning like a merry-go-round, by itself. God is not a person, like an architect who designs and builds the universe and then rests. God is not like a painter who paints a picture and then leaves it and goes to do something else. God is more like a dancer.

You cannot separate the dancer from the dance. In India you see many temples of dancing Shiva. What it signifies is that creation is a continuous dance, an ongoing process rather than an event. We, humans and non-humans, are all gods: we all partake in the continuous creation as well as the continuous dissolution of the world. God is existential reality: the principle of mutuality, reciprocity and relatedness. According to this existential principle, we humans and non-humans are eternally engaged in the dance of co-evolution and co-creation.

We all have the ability to use our imaginations to appreciate the divine presence in every moment. However, it seems to me that we have almost completely lost our divine imagination. Since your mother was so strongly rooted in the divine imagination, please tell me how she brought you up to be a pilgrim.

Yes, I was very fortunate to have a mother who was extremely wise. She saw nature as divine. She taught me to connect with nature because we *are* nature, and therefore we are related to everything around us.

The word nature, *natura* in Latin, means birth. Natal, nativity, and nature come from the same root. Native refers to the place of birth. Whatever is born is nature. So nature is not just out there. Trees, birds, animals, mountains and rivers are considered to be nature, but we humans see ourselves as separate from nature. How can this be? Are we not born? Of course we are, so we are nature too. In our arrogance we even think that we are superior to nature, which is a mistake. My mother taught me to revere nature, and to feel one with nature. What I do to nature I do to myself, because I am nature.

When I walked with my mother to the farm, she would always point to the mysteries of the natural world. The honey bee was one of her favourite subjects. She would watch the honey bees gathering nectar and returning to their hives. She would say, "Look at the honey bee. The honey bee can teach us the lesson of transformation." Now that is the divine dimension. The honey bee is a physical reality, performing a physical action, but there is an invisible reality. A process of creation and transformation is taking place. The honey bee goes from flower to flower, collecting nectar. A little from here, a little from there – never too much; no flower has ever complained that the honey bee took too much nectar away! And once the bee has collected nectar, it transforms the nectar into sweet, delicious, healthy honey. This process of transformation is the divine dimension, alongside the practical, functional act of making honey. As George Herbert wrote,

Bees work for man; and yet they never bruise
Their Master's flower, but leave it, having done,
As fair as ever, and as fit to use;
So both the future doth stay, and honey run.

Bees are also pollinators, and that pollination is the key to our existence. If there are no bees, there is no pollination; if there's no pollination, there are no plants; if there are no plants, there is no food; if there's no food, there's no life. This is a clear example of how all life is interconnected and interdependent. My mother's conviction was that all is in one and one is in all. As William Blake wrote:

To see a world in a grain of sand, and heaven in a wild flower,
Hold infinity in the palm of your hand and eternity in an hour.

This is how my mother taught me to be a pilgrim in nature. Being a pilgrim in nature is being one with the divine. By connecting with nature I realise that everything is intricately and completely interdependent. Life will not exist if there are no bees; this shows how the macrocosm is in the microcosm, and the microcosm in the macrocosm.

To be a pilgrim is to be connected. We are all connected, we are all related, there is no I and the other, I am the other, the other is me – that is what makes me a pilgrim of life and a pilgrim of the Earth. My pilgrimage is not going somewhere; my pilgrimage is to be one with the universe. I am the universe, and the universe is me. When I come out of my narrow identity, out of this limited sphere of my personality, my ego-self, and see my body not as separating me from the rest of the world but as connecting me with the world, then I am a pilgrim. The universe is my home; even when I am walking I am at home!

The universe is made of many elements, including earth, air, fire, water, space, time, imagination and intelligence. Human beings have all of these elements in a miniature form, in a microcosm. If we can realise that, then we can know we are the universe. That's the self-realisation that a Buddha, a Jesus Christ or a Lao Tsu achieves. They become the universe by realising that they are the universe.

When I see in me the rivers of the world flowing, the mountains of the Earth standing, the forests growing, the sun, moon and stars shining' when I see that all manifestations are in me and I am in them, then I become the mind of god, the cosmic mind, the universal consciousness.

Is there a simple way to attain such consciousness?

Walking is a way. When I walk I touch the Earth, and Earth holds the mind of god. When I am walking I have time – I am going slowly. And when I am going slowly, then I am looking around. I can sense the sacred all around me. Life is sacred. Honey bees are sacred. Trees are sacred. Life is sacrificing life to maintain life. That is what makes life sacred. If I am on horseback, or worse in a car or a train, or worst of all in an aeroplane, I see little. I don't connect. But when I am walking I am connected with the Earth, with the air, with the trees, with the sunshine, with the flowers, with the fungi, with the birds, I am connected with the entire universe. There is no dualism, I am completely one with the universe, attuned. This is why pilgrims mostly go on foot.

I walk in nature, not as an escape from the strain and stress of urban life, not for entertainment or sightseeing, not even as a scientist looking at nature as an object of study. I go as a pilgrim for the renewal of my spirit. Walking in nature is my meditation and my prayer. The magnificent trees and majestic hills are my temples and cathedrals. I don't look above the sky to seek heaven; my heaven is here on Earth. Being one with nature, I am enchanted and enlightened.

Walking makes the journey itself the destination; there is no destination outside the journey. When you are walking you can look at the flowers and appreciate them; look at the bees and learn from them; nature becomes your teacher, your mentor, your guide, your guru and your god; all are one!

As a pilgrim on foot I can observe nature and connect with her on a deeply spiritual level. A tourist takes a picture with a camera; a pilgrim takes a picture with the heart.

Pilgrims also seem to have a place of pilgrimage towards which they are heading. Why is that? What are they seeking?

I don't know about other pilgrims. Every pilgrim has his or her own purpose. For me, there is no destination, there is nowhere to go, nothing to achieve, nothing to seek; all is here. I am only participating in the process of the sacred universe, celebrating, delighting, and being. Every step is a place of pilgrimage. Of course, it is a useful pretext to undertake a journey with a destination in mind. For example, I took a pilgrimage to Mount Kailash and also to Santiago de Compostela. Journeying to such sacred destinations is a helpful inspiration to get me out of my home and bring me into a challenging and vivid relationship with the world. I welcome this practical and down-to-earth motivation, but at the same time I have to let go of the desire to arrive, and yield to the joy of sacred drift.

Of course your longest and greatest pilgrimage, an inner pilgrimage as well as an outer pilgrimage, was the walk you undertook from India to America. You were only 26 years old then.

The inspiration for this walk came from Bertrand Russell, the 90-year-old Nobel Prizewinner Lord Russell. While he was protesting against nuclear weapons he was arrested and put in a British jail for breaking the law and "disturbing the peace of the Queen"!

When I read this news I was amazed. At that time I was in a café with a friend and I said to my friend E. P. Menon: "Look, here is a man of 90 going to jail for trying to bring about peace in the world! And what are we doing, just sitting here drinking coffee? Let's do something for peace, for Bertrand Russell, for the Earth." We talked and talked, and in the end we decided to walk to Moscow, Paris, London and Washington DC, the four nuclear capitals of the world. We felt very excited and happy.

Our guru, Vinoba Bhave, gave us his blessings and said: "If you are making a peace pilgrimage of the Earth, then go without money in your pockets. The root cause of war is fear. To make peace you have to eliminate fear and harbour trust in your heart. When you have money you can think that money will protect you and support you. But when you have no money you have to trust yourself, you have to trust people and you have to trust god."

"Without any money?" I asked in surprise.

"No money at all," said Vinoba. "Otherwise, when you are walking you will be tired and exhausted so you will go to a restaurant to eat and find a guest house to sleep in. The next day you will walk away. But when you have no money you will be forced to find some kind person to give you hospitality, and that will open your channel of communication."

That was amazing advice! Just one thought changed the nature of our journey, and an outer journey was transformed into an inner journey.

This seems like very hard advice. Did you have to follow it?

Yes, we did.

In India the place of the guru is very important, and following the advice of the guru is an essential part of that relationship. One cannot be a dilettante about the relationship with your guru, one cannot say, "I will take the advice of the guru only if it suits me and only if I like it." To trust the world, you have to trust your guru. So my friend and I accepted Vinoba's advice.

We started walking from the grave of Mahatma Gandhi in New Delhi, and walked 8,000 miles to the grave of John F. Kennedy. That walking, across the continents, was a total antithesis to tourism.

When we reached the border of Pakistan, many of our friends, family members and colleagues gathered to bid us farewell.

One of my close friends was worried and afraid. He said:

"Aren't you mad to go through Pakistan on foot, without money and without food? Pakistan is our enemy country – we have had three wars between India and Pakistan! It is a Muslim country. I fear for your life. At least you should take some food with you!"

And he produced some packets of food and wanted to give them to me. I looked at the packets, and I was bewildered. I hesitated and thought for a moment, and suddenly heard an inner voice. I said to my friend:

"No, I cannot take food with me. You are very kind and generous to think of my welfare, but I will be betraying the advice of my guru if I carry food with me. These packets of food are not packets of food, they are packets of mistrust. What am I going to say to my Pakistani hosts? Am I going to say that I have brought my own food all the way from India because I did not know whether you would feed me or not? This is not a sign of trust. Please forgive me for refusing your kind gift, I am grateful, but I must adhere to my guru's teaching about trust. A pilgrim's journey is a journey of trust."

My friend was in tears, he gave me a big hug.

"But why are you crying my friend?" I asked.

"I don't know, Satish, if I will ever see you again! You are going through Muslim countries, Christian countries, capitalist countries, communist countries, through mountains, deserts, forests; you have no money, no food, no guidebook, no addresses. My heart goes out to you. I don't know if you will return to India alive."

I understood my friend's fear and feelings, but I said to him: "My dear friend, don't fear and don't worry. If I die walking for peace, that is the best kind of death one could wish for, so if I don't return alive, that is fine. But I must make this journey for peace in trust and please give me your love and blessing. He hugged me again, sobbing.

You left him crying?

Yes, I had to! I said goodbye to him and walked into Pakistan. To my utter surprise, within a few minutes of my entering into Pakistan, I heard someone calling our names:

"Are you Satish and Menon, the two Indians who are coming to Pakistan for peace?"

I could not believe my ears – it was like a miracle! I said:

"Yes we are, but we don't know anyone in Pakistan, we have written to nobody and here you are, you know our names! You know the purpose of our journey!"

"Yes, I heard about your journey from other travellers who have seen you walking from New Delhi to here. I also read about you in our papers. I said to myself, 'I am for peace. War between India and Pakistan is complete nonsense,' so I wanted to come and welcome you. Please come to my home and be my guests. I want you to meet my friends and my family and talk about peace. Please tell us how can we live together in peace?"

Now I was in tears. Five minutes ago my friend told me that I was going to an enemy country and here I was standing face to face with a so-called enemy, and this enemy wants peace! The idea of my identity of an Indian was shattered within seconds. I said to my friend Menon:

"If we come here as Indians we meet Pakistanis, if we come here as Hindus we meet Muslims, but if we come here as human beings we meet human beings. So from now on we will make our journey, not as Indians, not as Hindus, but as human beings – that is our primary identity. Indians, Hindus, Gandhians etc. etc. are just the identities of convenience, they are secondary. Let us not allow those identities to undermine our primary identity."

As Menon and I were talking our Pakistani host said:

"I live in Lahore, which is 16 miles from here. Please come with me in my car."

That request put us in a dilemma. We did not want to refuse his hospitality, but neither did we want to break our vow of only walking. So we said:

"We must walk, but please give us your address and we will certainly come to you by the evening."

He was reluctant to leave us, and said:

"How am I to know that someone else on the way will not offer you hospitality? I don't want to lose you. I have been coming here and searching for you for days. I came here yesterday and the day before yesterday, looking for you. I was wondering whether you had crossed the border somewhere else. Then I thought, there is no other border to cross, all other borders are closed. So I came today and I am so happy to find you. Now I don't want to lose you!"

"No, we won't accept anyone else's offer of hospitality because you are the first to invite us; but we must walk, for that is our vow. That is the way of the pilgrim. Touching the Earth is the first step towards peace."

Instantly our host had a brilliant idea. He said:

"It is hot, and you don't want to carry your rucksacks on your backs. It is better for you to walk light – so please let me take your rucksacks in my car? That way I will be assured that, at least to collect your bags, you will come to my house."

We laughed; what a good idea! So we gave our rucksacks to our host, and began our journey by stepping on the soil of Pakistan.

In the evening, as we were approaching the gorgeous Garden of Shalimar, just on the outskirts of Lahore, our host appeared, walking towards us: "It will be difficult for you to find my house, so I thought I would come to meet you and guide you through the streets of Lahore."

On the very first day of our journey outside India, trust gave birth to peace and friendship between two Indians and a Pakistani family.

Was this an exceptional, first-day miracle, or did you also find such friendship later in your journey?

No, this was not an exception – the experience was repeated again and again. We walked through villages, towns and cities, we walked through fields, forests, hills and mountains; we walked in the night under the moonlight, we walked in the cool of the morning and also in the evening. We rested during the day, escaping from the heat of the sun. Sometimes we rested under the trees, and sometimes in the shade of roadside restaurants.

One day, as we were climbing the 4,000-feet-high Khyber Pass, a car passed us. Then it stopped and it reversed, stopping near us. The driver, not a Pakistani, but a white man kindly asked:

"Do you want a lift?"

We felt a sense of gratitude for such a kind offer, but we stuck to our vow and said:

"No thank you, we are walking."

The driver was puzzled; perhaps he couldn't believe that we would refuse a lift in such an inhospitable place. He asked:

"Where are you walking to? I am going all the way to Kabul. I can drop you wherever you are going."

Hearing the American accent, I lightheartedly said:

"As a matter of fact we are walking to the United States of America!"

The driver was even more puzzled, and also intrigued. He actually got out of the car and said:

"Gentlemen, do you know where the United States of America is?"

Smiling, I said:

"We have never been there, but we believe that America exists. We have seen it on the map, and we hope to discover it!"

The driver said:

"I don't believe you will make it to America by walking, but here is my business card. My phone number is on it. If you ever reach the shores of the USA, please give me a ring – I will want to know that you have made it."

We thanked him and kept the card safely. When one has no money, an address card is very useful!

We walked to the border of Afghanistan, over the Hindu Kush mountains and into the deserts of Herat, and then into the even more dusty, dry and desolate desert of Iran. After 100 days of walking in Iran we walked through Azerbaijan, Armenia and Georgia, along the Black Sea to the north, to Moscow, then Poland, Germany, Belgium and France. Up to here there had been no water to cross, but in Calais we were faced with the English Channel, so a kind French lady said:

"You cannot cross the Channel on foot and you have no money, so here are two tickets for the ferry."

Thus we crossed the Channel from Calais to Dover, and walked to London. At long last we met Bertrand Russell, the 92-year-old grand old man of Peace. We had written to him from India, when we were starting our journey, so when we met him he said:

"When I received your letter I did not believe that I would be alive to see you!" Then he laughed, and said: "But you have walked fast enough, and I am pleased to be able to meet you."

After a long conversation and after we had narrated many of our stories from the journey, Bertrand Russell made a very practical point:

"I wish you well in reaching Washington DC. However, you have no money and you cannot walk on water! Can we help you and arrange a flight to Washington for you?"

"It is kind of you, but we do not wish to fly. From walking to flying is too big a jump! But we would be very grateful if you would arrange two boat tickets for us to New York. Then we will walk from New York to Washington."

Bertrand Russell and other peace activists in Britain got us two tickets for the Queen Mary – a luxurious boat with a comfortable cabin to ourselves, and we crossed the Atlantic in seven days. The boat was so big that we could easily keep up our practice of walking – up and down, and around the decks – and in due course we arrived in New York.

En route from New York to Washington we came to the city of

Philadelphia, where the kind driver we had met in the Khyber Pass lived. His name was Dr Scarf, and when we arrived in the city we phoned him:

"Do you remember the two Indians you met in the Khyber Pass?"

"Yes, I do. Where are they?"

"We are right here, in your city. We have made it. It took us two years; it was a slow journey, and slow is peaceful."

He was thrilled to hear from us and invited us to his house. He got many of his friends together, cooked a delicious vegetarian dinner and said to his friends: "When I met these two Pilgrims I thought they were crazy and that they would never make it to America. But I am happy to be proven wrong. I am impressed with the resilience of their human spirit."

What an incredible story! Then what happened? Did you continue the journey?

Yes, we walked to Washington DC, and ended our journey at the grave of John F. Kennedy; from the grave of Gandhi to the grave of Kennedy; from grave to grave – graves made by the bullets of assassins, graves made as a consequence of a violent culture. As long as we have faith in the gun there will be the premature deaths of heroes such as Gandhi and Kennedy. The gun does not only kill the bad guys; it can also kill the good guys. The so called 'good guys', like the members of armed forces or the police, try to kill the bad guys, and the bad guys try to kill the good guys. But there is no such thing as good on one side and bad on the other. Good and bad go through every human heart. Through the gun we water the seeds of violence. When we stop watering the seeds of violence we will have peace.

We cannot make peace in the human world unless we make peace with the Earth, peace with nature. Humans and nature are not two separate entities – humans are nature. Human life and other-than-human life are part of one single web of life. I realised this unity of life by walking the Earth.

Did you meet the world leaders and policy-makers?

Yes, we met some of them. We had a particular reason to reach out for them.

When we were walking along the Black Sea we met two Russian women. We gave them a leaflet about our peace pilgrimage in the Russian language which explained why we were walking and where we were going. The Russian women read our leaflet and asked us:

"Have you truly walked all the way from India?"

"Yes, indeed, we have."

"How amazing! A Russian saint, Rasputin, went from Russia to India. Your travels sound like a return journey!"

"Thank you for that comparison!" We smiled.

"We work here in this tea factory. This is our lunch break, so please come and have a cup of tea and tell us the story of your walk."

"Of course – any time is tea time."

So we went in, the women brought us cups of tea and some bread and cheese, and we started to talk. We could speak a little bit of Russian, and there was someone there who could interpret us as well. As we were deeply engaged in conversation, one of the women had a brilliant brainwave. She went out of the room and came back with four packets of tea, which she gave to us, saying:

"These packets of tea are not for you. If you want some tea I can give you some other packets."

"Who are they for, then?", we asked.

"I would like you to be my peace messengers, and to deliver one packet of this peace tea to our premier in Moscow, the second to the president of France in Paris, the third to the prime minister of England in London, and the fourth packet to the president of the United States of America in Washington. Please give them a message from me."

"What is your message?"

"My message to them is this, 'If you ever get a mad thought of pressing the nuclear button, please stop for a moment and have a fresh cup of tea from this packet of Peace Tea. That will give you a moment to stop and reflect that nuclear weapons will not only kill your enemies, for they will kill innocent men, women and children, and they will destroy forests, rivers, lakes and mountains. They are not just weapons of war – they are weapons of total annihilation. They will eliminate animals, birds and bees. They are weapons to bring an end to life, so do not use them.' "

What an inspiring message! From that day on we became the ambassadors of two Russian women, carrying their message and the packets of Peace Tea. We delivered the first packet in the Kremlin, where we were received warmly by the President of the Supreme Soviet on behalf of the Russian Government. However, when we wanted to deliver the second packet to President De Gaulle in Paris, we were refused. So we went to the Palais Elysée and demanded to meet either the president himself or his representative to receive the packet of Peace Tea sent by the Russian women.

"The president has no time for peaceniks such as you. Please go away! In any case it is illegal to demonstrate in front of the Palais Elysée; you are breaking the law," we were told.

"We are not going to go away; we will stand here until we have delivered the Peace Tea," we said.

Within half an hour of our being there we were arrested and taken to a dreadful dungeon. However, we were happy to be there, thinking of our mentor Bertrand Russell, whose imprisonment had inspired us in the first place. We were following in his footsteps. After three days in jail we were met by the Indian Ambassador and the Chief of the French Police.

"The police officer will receive your Peace Tea and ensure that it will be delivered to the Palais Elysée," said the Indian Ambassador. "I am sure you will wish to continue with your journey and not stay in jail here. Otherwise the French Government may deport you back to India. You would not wish to be in such a situation!"

We agreed, and thus were released. We managed to be received by a representative of the British Government in the House of Commons, with the promise that the Peace Tea would remain at 10 Downing

Street for such an eventuality. Similarly we were received in the White House in Washington by a representative of the President. Thus we, the pilgrims, became messengers of peace.

Our journey had a particular purpose, and all journeys can have their own individual meaning and motivation. However, every journey is a journey to connect with people, to connect with the planet and to connect with oneself.*

---

* The full story of this peace pilgrimage, as well as other pilgrimages undertaken by the author are described in greater detail in the author's autobiography No Destination, also published by Green Books.

Chapter Two

WE ARE ALL RELATED

Though with great difficulty I am got hither, yet now I do not repent me of all the trouble I have been at to arrive where I am. My sword I give to him that shall succeed me in my pilgrimage, and my courage and skill to him that can get it. My marks and scars I carry with me, to bear witness for me that I have fought his battles who will now be my rewarder. . . . So he passed over and the trumpets sounded for him on the other side.

John Bunyan, *The Pilgrim's Progress* (Mr Valiant-for-Truth)

The story of your pilgrimage for peace is spellbinding, but can we go back a bit? We were talking about your mother. She was illiterate, yet wise. She seems to be like a natural pilgrim. Where did she get her wisdom from?

The traditional society of India is connected with the spirit, with the soul, and with the Earth. My mother's ancestors lived in this way, close to the land; they derived their livelihood from the natural world, living with intimate knowledge of their local ecosystem, feeling themselves connected with the biosphere. They did not live in high-rise buildings, or air-conditioned houses, or move about in fast cars – all these boxes and compartments that we have built around us. My mother's wisdom was received through oral tradition, oral culture, passed on from one generation to another.

My mother could neither read nor write; she could not even put her signature on legal papers, so she used her thumbprint for that purpose. But she was educated; illiterate, but educated. And even more, she was wise, she was a very conscious being because she was connected with the Earth, with nature. So her wisdom came from her ancestors and from her intimate connection with plants, soil, insects, animals, and humans. She may not have read the great books of the world, but she read the book of nature. Moreover she was a child of the great Indian oral tradition, where knowledge and wisdom are passed down through songs, stories and myths, learned by heart and remembered throughout life. My mother sang the devotional songs of the Rajasthani poet-pilgrim Sister Mira, a wandering ascetic revered by Muslims and Hindus alike. My mother was a great storyteller too, and she narrated to me the epic stories of the Ramayana and

Mahabharata, where gods, animals, humans, birds, forests and rivers are all entangled and interact.

When I think of my mother, I wonder at the assumption of so many people that illiteracy is a curse, a sign of backwardness, a limitation; for how many literate people know hundreds of songs, or can tell the great stories by heart? Misguided by the notion that literacy is synonymous with culture and civilisation, we have become confused and lost the traditional ways of knowing.

How is it that the majority of people in the world have pretty much lost sight of the value of different ways of knowing? How is it that the modern world has forgotten what is essential in traditional cultures?

We have forgotten because we have become one-dimensional. We seem to think that there is only one way to know, the intellectual way, whereas my mother believed that there are many ways of knowing. The one-dimensional way of knowing, prevalent in the modern world, is to know through measuring, through quantifying. This is the empirical approach: "That which cannot be measured does not matter." People even think that what cannot be measured does not exist. This reduces all kinds of knowledge to a limited methodology of literalism and materialism.

But there are many ways of knowing; emotional ways, spiritual ways, psychological ways, relational ways, sensual ways and experiential ways. If we embrace the idea that there are many ways of knowing, then our knowledge will be more comprehensive. We will know by measuring, by feeling, by loving, by doing, by making, and by experiencing. Intellectual knowledge, spiritual knowledge, traditional knowledge, and imaginative knowledge passed through the fire of experience bring wisdom and even enlightenment. A solely intellectual and empirical knowledge might make us clever, but our achievements will be limited.

There is nothing wrong with intellectual and empirical knowledge, as long as we do not discard other ways of knowing. So traditional societies – the aboriginal people of Australia, American Indians, Bushmen in Africa, Hindus in India, Taoists in China, Shintos in Japan – all had many ways of knowing, and therefore their knowledge was much more comprehensive and complete than our purely empirical knowledge system. Traditional societies were able to connect themselves with the universe through arts, crafts and stories, and through hunting, gathering, vision quests and rituals.

This way of knowing is missing from modern education. Scientific knowledge has become very powerful, at the expense of other ways of knowing. Modern educationalists are using this methodology in schools, in universities and in research departments. Everybody is being educated this way because people who are not educated in this way are considered backward or underdeveloped. The sign of development is that everybody goes to school, everybody becomes literate. Such schooling and literacy would present no problem if the teaching in schools and universities was not one-dimensional, but I am afraid that the modern education produces tourists rather than pilgrims!

What, then, is the multi-dimensional education which will produce pilgrims?

The word education comes from the Latin term *educare*, which implies that a teacher draws out what is best in you. All of us have intellect, emotions, artistry, imagination and spirit. Educators should address all of these aspects and bring out each person's unique genius, rather than seeing students as empty pots to be filled up with external information. Like a gardener helps and encourages the plant to emerge from the seed, in the same way a teacher helps and encourages students to realise their potential.

There are three ways to learn: to know with our minds, to experience with our hearts, and to practise with our bodies. If we only know something in our heads, but do not experience nor practise what we know, then a head is no more than a dictionary, an encyclopaedia or a store of information.

There is a lovely story in the Mahabharata. When Yudhishtira, the eldest brother of the five Pandava princes, was a child, he was given a Sanskrit lesson by his teacher.

"I give you three lines to learn by heart:
Speak the truth,
Follow the right path,
Do not succumb to anger.
Please learn this verse by tomorrow morning."

Next day when Yudhishtira arrived at the class, the teacher asked him,
"Have you learned your three lines?"
"Sir, I have learned two lines:
Speak the truth
Follow the righteous path
But, I am sorry, I still haven't learned the third line."
"You must be a dull student! I give you another day. I want to hear no excuses. By tomorrow I want all three lines learned by heart and properly pronounced."

The next day, the teacher again asked Yudhishtira,
"Have you learned your lines?"
"Sir, I am sorry, but I still have not learned the third line."
"You are the most stupid student I have ever come across! What's the matter with you? Such a short line, and yet you have failed to learn it. I give you a last chance. Tomorrow you must come having learned the line."

On the third morning, the teacher asked in exasperation,
"Yudhishtira! How about your lines, have you learned them?"
Yudhishtira shook his head sadly, and in an apologetic voice said,
"Sir, I am very sorry for being so slow, I am still trying without success."
The teacher became extremely angry, and spoke in a harsh voice,

"You are not trying hard enough, so you should be expelled from the class", and overcome with rage, he slapped Yudhishtira on the face.

Yudhishtira stood still, breathing calmly. After a few moments' pause he said, "Sir! I have learned the third line – Do not succumb to anger."

The teacher was amazed. "How could this be? Just a moment ago you said you had not learned, and now you have learned!"

"Sir, you slapped me on the face, yet I was not angry, so at last I have learned – not to succumb to anger."

Learning is not just an academic exercise: it is also experiencing and practising. And practising is not merely acquiring techniques and skills in order to get a job and earn money. Practising is to live your daily life according to the perennial principles of harmony, humility and love. That is the pilgrim's view of education.

Modern schooling is far from the essential meaning of education. In the name of education, everyone is being brainwashed throughout the world. Everywhere there is only one methodology – my friend Vandana Shiva calls it *monoculture of the mind*. Modern India, modern Japan, modern Europe, modern America, modern Australia – all are following the *modernity* of monoculture. We are all conditioned into thinking that only quantitative and materialistic education matters. If we want an ecological, sustainable, spiritual, fulfilling, joyful, happy and self-realised life, then we have to expand and broaden our ways of knowing. We have to be more inclusive, we have to stop saying *"There is only one right way, and that's the scientific way. All other ways are wrong."* This is a form of scientific fundamentalism, which is prevalent in our modern education. We have to be free of this scientific fundamentalism. We have to realise that the scientific way is one way; it's a useful way, it's a good way, but there are other ways as well. Other ways are intuitive, experiential, based in caring, loving and being compassionate. These are ways based in spirituality, which are also good ways of knowing and making sense of the world.

The aim of traditional education was to find the meaning of life, whereas modern education is a kind of brainwashing to get a well-paid job and earn as much money as possible!

This brainwashing is a serious situation. Thanks to that, everybody wants to have a car, a house, a refrigerator, an insurance policy, holidays abroad. . . . If six billion people on this planet Earth were to live such a lifestyle, then we would require three or four planet Earths. That is not going to happen. We're not going to get even one new Earth! And because of brainwashing, people are not going to give up their refrigerators, their cars and their lifestyles. People who believe in science and progress and technology are not going to suddenly change because of some amorphous theory of everything being interconnected. This is the challenge that we face. The best way to meet this challenge is to move from quantitative education to qualitative and holistic education.

The modern consumerist lifestyle has consequences, for there is no such thing as a lifestyle that is free of consequences. They are threefold: stress on the individual, stress on society and stress on the environment. If you have cars, computers, televisions and all the other paraphernalia, but no happiness, no genuine relationships, no friendships, no family life, then what is the good of all those cars and computers? So at this moment many, many people are realising that "I have all the things I need, yet I'm not happy. So how can I create a new life that is simple, but nourishing? How can I develop an elegant simplicity, where authentic relationships are at the core of my life."

The opposite of simplicity is glamour, consumerism and fashion – which is the antithesis of sustainability. Many of our economic and environmental problems are the consequence of our desire to show off, to impress. I call it a 'tourist mentality'. We are obsessed by our egos, and the desire for glamour has become a world problem. As Oscar Wilde said, "Fashion is a form of ugliness, so intolerable that we have to alter it every six months"!

What you are saying is that pilgrims practise simplicity in life.

Simplicity is part of the 'perennial wisdom' promoted by many great thinkers and visionaries. Although sometimes people think simplicity means a kind of 'hair shirt' lifestyle, that is not my view. Simplicity is a positive quality; when things are simple they are well-made, they are made to last, they are made with pleasure and they give pleasure when used. It was E. F. Schumacher who said that "Any fool can make things complicated, but it requires a genius to make things simple."

Simplicity requires less ego and more imagination, less complication and more creativity, less glamour and more gratitude, less attention to appearance and more attention to essence.

Trendy, fashionable consumer-oriented lifestyles are the cause of a threefold crisis. The first is the environmental crisis, where over-exploitation of resources causes climate change. The second is the social crisis, where resources are appropriated by the few, and large numbers of people are deprived of their essential rights, which causes poverty and social injustice. The third is the spiritual crisis: the crisis of disconnection and loneliness. Consumerism and addiction to 'fast-fashion' undermine the values of friendship, family, neighbourliness and humility.

Simplicity is not about looking backwards or turning the clock back to a pre-industrial past. Elegant simplicity is about a post-industrial future where technology is at the service of the Earth and humanity. We can benefit from our scientific and technological discoveries without compromising ecological, social and spiritual integrity. Progress without principles, science without spirituality, consumerism without conscience, money without morality and knowledge without wisdom destroy social cohesion and human relationships. When we move away from simplicity and focus on the accumulation of more and more material as well as non-material possessions, we lose the centrality of human relationships, and loneliness results.

The backbone of human life is good relationships. Without the backbone you cannot hold the body up. You need your flesh, your nervous system, hair, hands, feet and all other parts of the body. But if there is no backbone, the body will not stand up; it will fall apart. So what is the backbone of human life? Good relationships with your fellow human beings: with your partner, your children, your mother, your father, your neighbours, your friends. As they say in French, *"Les relations humaines sont les plus précieux."* And, of course, a good relationship with the natural environment – with the land, with the animals, with the trees, with the place where we live – is equally essential.

Only through relationships can we reach a sense of fulfilment and joy. One is most happy when one is in relationship. Modern lifestyle is destroying the fundamentals of relationships. The consequence of a materialistic, acquisitive, fashionable, consumerist lifestyle is bringing gross unhappiness. And that gross unhappiness is the price that we are paying, on a personal level.

We are also paying a price on the social level, for the modern lifestyle is causing a great deal of social injustice. In cities like Tokyo, Hong Kong and New York there is tremendous wealth alongside terrible slums. There is a very unfair housing system whereby on the one hand some people live in luxurious apartments, and on the other hand a much larger number of people are forced to live in shanty towns and on the streets because all the resources are sucked away by the few.

Then there are environmental consequences. We are using huge amounts of fossil fuel to run our energy systems, our industry, our shopping, our food distribution systems, and in the production of clothing, shoes, furniture, computers, televisions – everything we are producing and consuming is based on one source of energy: oil. We use millions of barrels of it every day. One consequence of such consumption is global warming, and the other is global wars.

If we start to look at the consequences of our modern lifestyle, we will realise that they are not very happy ones. So a fundamental change in our collective way of life is a personal, social and environmental imperative. These systems on which modern life is based were built by humans, and can be changed and rebuilt by humans – there is nothing inevitable about them. If our systems are damaging personal, social and environmental coherence, then we need to redesign those systems, and such redesigning requires a new consciousness: an eco-logical consciousness, a spiritual consciousness.

When people see this, and make the connections between their own lifestyle and the negative consequences that result when it is reproduced on a global scale, then I think they will welcome a redesigning of the world, and a lifestyle which is elegant, simple, comfortable, beautiful, joyful and happy. If we redesign the world in a way that is personally, socially and environmentally satisfying, then we will not need three or four planets. We can live on one planet happily. "There is enough in the world for everybody's need, but not enough for anybody's greed," said Gandhi. So we have to redesign the world on the basis of need and rela-tionships rather than on the basis of greed and fragmentation. This task of redesigning our systems begins with education.

To some extent that is what you are doing at Dartington.

The history of Dartington Hall as a centre of education, rural regener-ation and culture is that it was established in 1926, by an Englishman, Leonard Elmhirst, and his American wife Dorothy. Leonard had worked in India with Rabindranath Tagore, the Nobel prizewinning poet who had established a school which he called "the poet's school" and named it *Shantiniketan* (house of peace). When Leonard returned to England, full of inspiration, he and Dorothy bought a run-down medieval manor house in Devon. The estate included a thousand acres of land on the banks of the river Dart, by the village of Dartington.

In time they established a primary school, a secondary school, a col-lege of arts, various craft workshops and a working farm. Thus Dartington Hall became a well-known experiment in the liberal arts, progressive education and what was then considered scientific farming.

In 1979 Maurice Ash, then chairman of the Dartington Hall Trust, persuaded me to come and live in Devon. In 1990 we established Schumacher College in order to carry on the work of Tagore and the

Elmhirsts, but in the context of our own time, when the issues of the environment and the ecological crisis are paramount. We named the college after the economist E. F. Schumacher, the author of *Small is Beautiful*, who had linked spiritual values with the economy in his famous essay on *Buddhist Economics*. Schumacher was perhaps the first Western economist to put those two words together; Buddhism and economy and show the link between idealism and pragmatism.

Thus the activities of Schumacher College and Dartington Hall rest on the foundations laid by Tagore and the Elmhirsts.

Most university education is disconnected: science is not related to economics, economics is not related to politics, and politics is not related to anything else; all the subjects are put in separate boxes, separate departments. So we created a college where education is transdisciplinary. Ecology connects with economics, science connects with spirituality, politics connects with daily life.

Economics and ecology share the same etymological roots in the Greek word '*oikos*'. '*Oikos*' means 'home'. '*Logos*' means knowledge. '*Nomos*' means management. Ecology is the knowledge of home, and economy is the management of home. To take care of anything you have to know it, understand it, and then you will be able to manage it well. If you don't know your home, how are you going to manage it? If you don't know where your living-room, kitchen, bathroom and bedroom are, or where your garden is, how are you going to put furniture and tools in the appropriate places? Therefore, knowledge of the home is essential in order to manage it.

But 'home' is not just the bricks and mortar, not just a building – it is more than purely a house. It is a place of relationships. When one says, "I am going home," it means "I'm going to the place where I have relations. My father, my mother, my daughter, my son, my wife, my husband, live there with me." Wherever your relations are, that's your home. In the context of ecology, home is the Earth itself, where humans, animals, mountains and forests are in relationships. All species, humans and other-than-humans are members of this planet home, this Earth family, this Earth community.

Ecology and economy should go together, like walking on two legs. If you were to walk almost exclusively on one leg – just the leg of economy – you would be limping. At the moment our society is limping because we have no knowledge or understanding of our planet home. That is why our economy is in such a mess, causing much distress.

Schumacher College connects ecology with economy; it is a place where knowledge is studied and developed in a holistic and interconnected way. Here learning and living go together, with everyone participating in meditation, in cooking, and in gardening. Science, philosophy and politics are studied together. The College is not just an academic centre, it is a living community. Monasteries operate in a similar way. Although Schumacher College is not a monastery, it is an 'ecostery'. People here can live and learn in an atmosphere of 'free spirit'.

We have short courses and also a one-year programme in Holistic Science. We organise our studies in such a way that education is responsive to the world situation. The purpose of education at the College is to serve the Earth, serve people and enhance relationships.

People often think that the purpose of education is to provide training so that students are able to earn a living. Can people who have studied at Schumacher College find jobs?

Earning a living is only a small part of education. Of course a truly educated person discovers his or her vocation, which should lead them to find a right livelihood: work which does not damage or deplete the natural world, which does not exploit other human beings, and which is not stressful to oneself. A livelihood is very different from a job or an employment. Jobs and employment are generally about having an income, rather than being a source of fulfilment; whereas a livelihood includes both fulfilment and an income. So my hope is that Schumacher students find a livelihood rather than a job.

Ecologically sustainable and spiritually fulfilling livelihoods are to be found mostly in the spheres of the arts, crafts, agriculture, and service to society. I am passionate about the arts and crafts. I would like to see all schools and universities teaching practical skills: gardening, cooking, building, pottery, woodwork, painting, poetry, dance and music. Through making we transform matter, and in turn matter transforms us. I call it the transformative power of arts and crafts. We can transform clay into a beautiful pot. We can take wood and transform it into a sculpture, or a chair. When we transform clay into beautiful pottery, we experience transformation. The clay goes through the fire of transformation, but we are also transformed. We are no longer who we were, now we are artists. We are potters or painters.

The potter Bernard Leach transformed clay, and clay transformed him. He became a potter of great vision and sensitivity. In Japan, the potter Shoji Hamada transformed clay into beautiful pots, and those beautiful pots transformed him. This experience of transformation can only happen when we are engaged with our hands, with our eyes, with our imagination. In the industrial mindset, we think that making things by hand is a sign of backwardness. "Only poor people make things – clever, rich people go into banking, finance and insurance, and work in big government offices." That kind of mindset needs to change, through education. At Schumacher College we are changing by engaging students and staff in gardening, cooking and other domestic activities. Daily activities are transformed into spiritual activities when they are performed mindfully, lovingly and caringly. When we give our full attention to the task in hand, it becomes part of our journey: it becomes a necessary part of our pilgrimage.

Our industrial culture of mass production is primarily concerned with function and fashion – rather than any sense of a spiritual and creative relationship with material objects. Our society is dominated by a utilitarian approach to everything.

There is nothing wrong with being a bit utilitarian, but not to the exclusion of other values such as beauty, joy, and reverence. My mother used to tell me that anything you make should have three dimensions. It should be beautiful, useful and durable. Beauty is essential, it is food for the soul. We are nourished when we are surrounded by beauty; flowers, pictures, pottery, tools; things well made bring us delight. Our houses, our clothes and our food should be beautiful. People in pre-industrial societies made shoes, jewellery, embroidery and everything else with tremendous care and skill. Now we collect those things in museums, and look at them with admiring eyes. Why are we not making similar objects of beauty ourselves?

In those times and cultures, beauty was not merely a matter of decoration, for objects of daily use were beautiful and useful at the same time. But even this is not enough, as things should also be durable. They should be made to last, so that resources are not used wastefully. Waste is a crime against nature. How would you like it if I wasted your time? You don't want me to waste anything of yours, yet we take things from nature and waste them. We create garbage and put it in landfill. Do you think nature likes this way that we act?

So these three aspects need to be present in the objects we make and use. I call it the 'BUD Principle'.

B – *Beautiful*
U – *Useful*
D – *Durable*

If we can follow the BUD principle every time we make something or acquire something, then we can be sure that we have a right relationship with the material world. This BUD principle could transform education if it was an integral part of school and university curriculums.

You talked about waste being a crime against nature. How can we change people's attitudes about this – for example about excess packaging?

We could be inspired by the Japanese tradition of the *furoshiki*, a beautiful piece of cloth for wrapping things, which is used and reused many times – for clothes, books, food and any other fairly small items. When you take them out you wash the *furoshiki*, and when you are giving a present to somebody, you wrap it in this cloth and use it again. That's an example of how to practise the BUD principle and avoid wasteful packaging.

In nature there is no waste. Nature has a wonderful system of packaging. Look at oranges: each segment is separately packaged, and they're bound together by tiny threads so they hold together. After that there is another packaging on the outside, the peel. When we put the peel on the compost, it becomes food for worms and for the soil. Thus we nourish the soil at the same time as eating an orange! Or take the cauliflower: it has the flower to eat, but it also has just as much greenery around it to protect the flower. When we want to eat, we take the greenery away and we put it in soup to make the stock, or we put it in the compost. But nowadays people put the orange peel or the cauliflower leaves into a plastic bag and put it in their waste bin. And what happens to the contents of the bin? A lorry comes and takes them to landfill.

Isn't it a crime against nature to take that nutrition away from worms and the soil? The orange peel and cauliflower leaves are there to replenish the soil, to nourish the soil, to nurture the worms, and we are putting all that into landfill where it will create greenhouse gases – yet we call ourselves intelligent, educated people! This shows how impoverished our education is.

Rather than working within the existing educational system, you have been involved in setting up new educational initiatives, including Schumacher College. Why is that?

It's no good just saying that the educational system is bad, the universities are bad, the schools are bad. We have to set up an alternative: it's better to light a candle than curse the darkness. There is no point in just criticising, blaming and condemning other systems. Why not take our energy, our creativity, our imagination, our effort and our time and do something different?

Schumacher College in an example of integrated learning. We have been especially successful in integrating science and spirituality. We have shown that these two can go together. Without spirituality, science can end up in all sorts of destructive technologies. It can become the victim of vested interests in business, the military, industry or government. In such circumstances science ends up creating nuclear weapons and GMOs (Genetically Modified Organisms), factory farms, wasteful production systems and so on. So science must be guided by spirituality.

At the same time, spirituality should be guided by science. If there is no science, no rational thinking, no intellectual consideration, then we end up with dogmatism and fundamentalism – whether Christian, Hindu or Islamic fundamentalism. This is the result of blind faith and blind thinking. So spirituality needs science, and science needs spirituality. We can have the best of both worlds if we marry science with spirituality. This is what we do at Schumacher College.

There's no point in being a pessimist. Old systems are dying. We need not moan about it; the old systems have had their day. Now it is time for them to collapse, so let them collapse. Our role is to be midwives to new systems. We must create new kinds of agriculture, new forms of education, new kinds of production systems, new health systems and so on. When this old, exploitative, wasteful, materialistic and dualistic paradigm comes to an end, we need to have new systems ready to replace the old.

Chapter Three

BEYOND GOOD AND EVIL

Forth, pilgrim, forth! Forth, beste, out of thy stal!
Know thy contry, look up, thank God of al;
Hold the heye way, and lat thy gost thee lede;
And trowth thee shall delivere, it is no drede.

Chaucer, *Truth, Balade de Bon Conseyle*, 1.18

The fragmentation you talked about did not exist, or not on the same scale, in indigenous, tribal cultures. Aboriginal cultures, native Americans, the shamanic cultures of the Amazon, the Bushmen of the Kalahari – all of these wonderful and fast disappearing tribal cultures had integrity.

Your comment reminds me of a Jain story:

Once upon a time Adam was lost in the jungle, where he encountered two wild elephants. They began to chase him. In order to escape from these frightening beasts Adam climbed a tall tree nearby, but the elephants were not going to let him go so easily; they curled their trunks around the tree and began to shake it furiously.

It so happened that above the branch Adam was holding was a beehive. As the tree shook, honey began to drip down, straight into Adam's mouth.

At that very moment some angels in their chariot were flying past, and seeing the desperate plight of Adam they slowed down and said:

"Come, we will rescue you, come into our chariot."

"Oh, how kind of you. But please let me have this sweet drop of honey, then I will come," said Adam.

The angels were kind and patient, and so they waited.

"All right, you've got your honey drop! Come now, be quick!"

"Please, let me have just one more drop," Adam pleaded.

The angels were astonished. They said,

"You are being stung by bees and any time now the elephants will pull the tree down. You greedy fool, you cannot let go of the desire for that drop of honey! Come, this is your last chance, come now or we will go."

"Please, please, let me have one more drop of honey – it is so delicious," said Adam.

The angels waited for a little while longer but in the end they could not draw Adam away from his imminent death and they left.

I think that the indigenous people are the angels of our time. They are calling on us to refrain from the momentary gratification of economic growth, which is like the honey drop.

The planet is threatened by global warming, rivers are polluted, rainforests are disappearing, human population is exploding, biodiversity is diminishing and traditional cultures are declining – all this in the pursuit of economic growth, so that we can have the sweet drops of consumption.

To sustain our desire to consume, we have created a world of monoculture. We have uniformity rather than unity, divisions rather than diversity. We seem to celebrate sameness – wherever we go we are confronted by the same kind of architecture, shopping centres, houses, foods, clothes and culture, education and entertainment. Behind the rhetoric of choice and competition, the government, businesses and industries promote monopoly, monoculture and sameness.

The vested interest of the established order is good at the use of sweet-sounding words such as liberty, freedom, democracy and sustainability; but their policies and actions lead to the concentration of economic and political power in fewer and fewer hands. Dignity, equity and equality are sacrificed at the altar of global greed.

Traditional cultures which do not fit within the paradigm of economic growth, commercial expansion, consumerism, globalisation and mass production are labelled at best as idealistic dreams. Traditional cultures are condemned as underdeveloped and backward. Systems of industrialisation, globalisation and centralisation are proclaimed as symbols of progress and development.

But one has to ask: where has this progress and development led us? What have the realists and pragmatists achieved? After 100 years of relentless destruction of nature and culture, where are we now? How can we take satisfaction in so-called progress and development while global wars, global warming and global poverty rage? How can we rejoice in the wealth of the few while millions of men, women and children suffer in hunger and deprivation? How can we rest when biodiversity and cultural diversity are constantly and dangerously under threat?

The time has come to stop and take stock, to look at the evidence and ask ourselves where we went wrong. In spite of the triumphs of science and technology, why do we live in the midst of multiple crises and conflicts?

In my view, the way forward is in the harmonious relationship between ecology and economy; between idealism and realism; between nature and culture; between environment and development; between tradition and progress; between unity and diversity; and, above all, we need to embrace the paramount importance of pursuing noble ends with noble means – let us join in the Dance of Diversity.

Let a thousand flowers bloom in the garden of Gaia. Let us celebrate the wisdom of traditional cultures and move sensitively towards the continual renewal of the human spirit.

Then how on Earth have we got so far off course, from those indigenous cultures? When and where did this fragmentation begin? Did it begin with the industrial revolution? Perhaps it did. Who was behind the industrial revolution? The Caucasian people, the white people, were behind the industrial revolution. Is there some kind of strange inherent fault line within the psyche of the Caucasian people? Having caused so many problems, one wonders whether the Caucasians are a source of evil?

The crisis we face is not due to the conflict of good and evil. Neither good nor evil are confined to a particular culture, country, colour, race or religion. Good and evil go through every human heart. The human heart and human mind are like a field. Every field contains seeds of flowers and weeds. Wisdom is to cultivate the flowers and discourage the weeds. In the same way, great teachers have taught humankind to root out the seeds of greed, craving, attachment, pride and anger, and the seeds of desire to dominate and control others. They encouraged us to cultivate the seeds of compassion, unity, generosity and feelings of relatedness.

The fact that the industrial revolution was initiated by the Caucasian race is in my view a historical coincidence. And somehow the Europeans managed to persuade and influence the rest of the world to follow their ways. The fact that India, China, Africa and some indigenous cultures have accepted the industrial mode of production and consumption shows that greed is not confined to the Caucasian race. At this stage I see no point in playing the blame game. Our challenge is to expose the fault line of the industrial mindset and persuade humanity to evolve into a holistic, natural and humane way of living.

The industrial revolution flourished in the soil of dualistic thinking. When we start to think of ourselves as separate individuals, atomised and autonomous beings, then we come to a view that "I am not you. I am not the tree. I am not the animals. I am a separate being." This separational worldview could be called evil, if you like, but it is only an ideology. However, this ideology has separated ecology from economy, and put the economy in charge of ecology. For indigenous people there was no separation between humans and nature, between ecology and economy. Many wise environmentalists are now saying that "the economy is a wholly owned subsidiary of ecology", but the economic paradigm which rules the world operates as if it were the other way around. Governments, industries and businesses, whether in the North, South, East or West – apart from a few enlightened exceptions such as in Bhutan – believe that the economy comes first. They believe that with economic growth it is possible to manage ecology and clean up the environment. This particular paradigm is at the root of the climate crisis and all the other problems you are talking about.

However, in reality ecology must come first. If there is no Earth well-being, there can be no human well-being. If there is no healthy Earth community, there can be no healthy human community. If there is no ecological capital then there can be no financial capital.

Financial capital is only an idea, a human device to make the exchange of goods and services easier – finance is basically a figure on a balance-sheet. The real capital is the Earth itself. As E. F. Schumacher said, "Nature is our true capital."

If the economy is growing but ecology is shrinking, then such economic growth is dangerously unsustainable. Growing the economy at the expense of ecology is *the* fundamental cause of global warming. If we want a sustainable future, if we want to solve the problem of climate change, the problems of hunger and poverty, then our first and foremost responsibility is to protect and maintain ecosystems such as the biodiverse rainforests and to promote ecological farming.

Unfortunately, the present economic paradigm has turned reality upside down. Economists, industrialists, bankers and financiers believe that money is wealth and nature is there to be transformed into figures on a balance-sheet. What does it matter if the forests have gone and the biosphere is polluted? As long as we have money, we can fix these problems one way or another. But money is not wealth; it is only a way of measuring human activities or the transactions of goods and services.

It is only in the past few hundred years that we have become so entangled with the system of money that we cannot imagine our existence without it. However, before the industrial revolution most societies, cultures and communities lived without banks, building societies, hedge funds and stocks and shares. But now money has become so central to our lives that nature has been turned into a commodity which can be bought and sold with money.

Moreover, 80% to 90% of the money swirling around the world day and night, moving from one account to another at the press of a button, has little connection to land, labour or goods; it is simply money chasing more money.

Should we get rid of money, then?

Not necessarily. There is nothing wrong with the idea of money in itself – it is a wonderful invention. It can make life very easy and convenient, as long as it serves the Earth community as well as the human community. But when humans and natural resources are sacrificed to the economy, then the balance of ecology and economy is destroyed.

Our efforts to reduce carbon emissions, necessary though they are, are of secondary importance. Carbon trading, finding alternatives to fossil fuels and other technological solutions should not become the reason for not taking the real steps of valuing and protecting the biosphere. Focusing only on carbon emissions without protecting ecosystems is merely treating the symptoms rather than addressing the root causes of global warming.

We seem to be in the grip of money. People and nature have become disposable in the interest of money. What can we do?

The world's money system is in need of a redesign. The system, which was created to facilitate economic transactions, is now creating economic tragedies. What was a measure of wealth has taken the place of wealth itself. What was a means to an end has now become an end.

As I said earlier, money is not wealth. It is a delusion to think that money is wealth. True wealth is good land, healthy animals, flourishing forests, clean water, honest work, abundant creativity and human imagination. Money was invented to oil the wheels of social interaction and to ensure that the relationship between natural resources and human needs was properly maintained.

The purpose of money was and should be to serve the human community as well as the Earth community. However, it appears that the original purpose has now been reversed. Instead of money serving the people and planet, now the people and the planet are put at the service of money. Natural resources are converted into consumables to make money. Whether these consumer goods are necessary or not is almost irrelevant. As long as money is made, all and everything can be justified; the money machine has to be kept in motion at all costs.

Of course, most of the money supply is controlled by the few; it may appear that there is never enough money to go around, but in fact there is plenty of money available to those who already have it. However, for the have-nots there is always a great scarcity. For example, there is never a shortage of finance for wars and weapons, but it is always in short supply for the arts and for education. There is no lack of money for producing fashionable goods for the rich, but never enough even for food for the poor. There never seems to be a problem in finding the money to build huge buildings for banks, supermarkets, office blocks, shopping centres and luxury villas, but there is never enough money to build houses for the poor.

There is a hierarchy in money. Some currencies are more valuable than others: the dollar dominates, the rouble is subservient. If you have euros, pounds and yen, you are privileged, but if you have only rupees or dinars you are disadvantaged. When you buy something with the dinar you need a hundred times more than you would, say, in dollars, and if you sell something you receive a hundred times less. If you work for a British bank in the UK your earnings are likely to be a hundred times greater than if you do the same job for the same bank in India. This is why telephone call centres have sprung up in poorer countries.

If you produce Nike shoes in Bangladesh you are paid a hundred times less than if you were producing the same pair of shoes in the USA. Thus money is an instrument of injustice and exploitation, not merely a means of exchange.

Money favours power, and power favours money. Modern democracy, in most countries, is government for the rich and by the rich. Money speaks louder than policies or personalities.

As John F. Kennedy once said, "What is designed by humans can be redesigned by humans." Money is not a god-given fixture; it was designed by us and therefore can be changed by us. Unless we reform and redesign our money system, the idea of sustainability, social justice and spiritual renewal will remain a mirage. Therefore the reform of the money system is an urgent imperative.

Your words are music to my ears. Failing banks, credit crunch, market meltdown, economic downturn – the financial crisis that the

world is facing at this moment means that it makes perfect sense to reform and redesign our money system. But is this enough to address our environmental problems, like the climate change of which most scientists are warning?

We have to look for holistic solutions. The credit crunch has shaken the stock-markets and banks around the world, but this is nothing compared with the impending crisis of a 'nature crunch'.

The credit crunch and nature crunch are related. Excessive greed and reckless lending, borrowing and spending are the cause of the credit crunch. We are doing the same with nature. Greedy pursuit of unlimited economic growth and wasteful use of environmental capital are risking the integrity and sustainability of the Earth itself. This will bring a nature crunch.

The unregulated and free-market financial systems encourage irresponsible speculation, unmanageable debt, rampant consumerism and the colossal waste of nature's gifts.

The banks and stock-markets and all our financial transactions are in the hands of highly educated, smart people who claim to be realists and intelligent. Then how have the banks managed to bring the whole system to the brink of disaster such that they have to go cap in hand to the government, begging to be bailed out?

The answer is staggeringly simple. The financial markets have turned the land, forests, rivers, animals and human creativity into commodities to be bought and sold, and even money itself has become a commodity – speculators trade in money to make more money.

We buy and sell houses, forests, foods and land to make money, and we buy and sell money to make money – almost everything has become a commodity, such that it is acceptable to engage in almost any kind of trading as long as it makes money. Money which was a means to trade has been turned into a status symbol, a source of power and prestige. This false philosophy of money is the root cause of the credit crunch and it will also lead to a nature crunch.

This nature crunch does not lie in the distant future; melting ice-caps and climate chaos are already with us, and that is because of our obsession with making money at all costs. We are over-fishing our oceans to make money, clear-cutting the rainforests, poisoning the land with chemical fertilisers, putting animals in factory farms, manipulating seeds with genetic engineering; the list goes on, and all this is to maximise money. We are prepared to let nature suffer, but not prepared to slow down the pace of economic growth. Money has a place within the broad context of sustainability and a harmonious relationship with the natural world but, we have to put it in its place and keep it there, rather than allow it to dominate our lives to such an extent that the human community as well as the Earth community is endangered.

As I have said, the cure for the credit crunch and the nature crunch is to put ecology before economy.

Recently I was invited to speak at the LSE, the London School of Economics. I asked my hosts, "You are a well-known university teaching economics, but where is your Department of Ecology?"

Their reply was, "We teach environmental studies as part of various other departments, but we do not have a Department of Ecology as such."

Now, the study of 'environment' is not the same as the study of 'ecology'. Environment is what surrounds us, the humans. The word implies that humans are at the centre and what is around us is our environment. Environment is an anthropocentric concept, whereas the word ecology is much more inclusive. The word implies relation-ships between all species, humans and other than humans.

What is taught at the LSE is only economy – the management of home – and not ecology, which is the knowledge of home. So from the perspective of an Earth Pilgrim's worldview, ecology should come before economy; knowledge before management. But at the LSE, as well as most other universities, economy dominates. These universi-ties are sending thousands upon thousands of young people into the world equipped with management skills but without the knowledge of what they are going to manage, these graduates are half-educated like half-baked bread, which is worse than being uneducated.

Together with ecology and economy we need a third 'E': ethics. Our 'oikos', our planet home, has to be built on the firm foundation of ethical and spiritual values, for without such a foundation our home will be unstable and unsustainable.

The credit crunch and nature crunch offer us a challenge and an opportunity to redesign our money system and our economics in such a way that we can restore the well-being of the human community as well as the Earth community. E. F. Schumacher's well-known essay on Buddhist Economics (which I mentioned earlier) and his book *Small is Beautiful* should be read again and again. He provided a vision of economics where people and planet mattered and where spiritual values underpinned economic values. Frugality, simplicity and restraint are the urgent imperatives at these critical times; if we are caring and generous to nature, nature will reciprocate.

You talk about frugality and simplicity as the solution to economic and environmental problems. But human desire for fashion, for nice things to show off, is natural. Do you object to such desires?

Yes I do. Many of our economic and environmental problems are the consequence of our desire to show off, to impress, to glitter and be obsessed with our ego self, so yes, the desire for glamour in itself is a world problem.

Once, when I was at the Economic Forum in Davos, the then President of South Africa, Thabo Mbeki, spoke about his dreams for the new South Africa, where everyone was able to own cars, computers and TV sets. From the floor I asked Mr Mbeki, "If people in South Africa, Brazil, China, India and the rest of the world attempt to own personal computers, cars, TV sets and the latest fashion in clothes, like the Europeans and Americans do, then we will need the resources of three or four planets. Mr President, we haven't got three or four planets; we have only one. Isn't it time for Europeans and Americans to free themselves from their obsession with fashion and consumer goods rather than Indians, Africans and Chinese aspiring to the wasteful Western lifestyle? Can we not design a lifestyle of elegant simplicity which is just, fair and sustainable?"

My question was heard in stunned silence. Mr Mbeki appeared to be taken aback for a moment; perhaps he was not expecting anyone in that gathering to question the quest for higher living standards. After a few seconds of reflection, he replied, "We cannot turn the clock back to an egalitarian, pastoral past; we are in the age of technology, progress and development. We cannot allow our people not to enjoy the same comforts and conveniences which European and Americans take for granted. I want to bring high living standards to our people in South Africa and I am sure governments in India and South America want to do the same. There are plenty of resources to go round!"

Of course, there was no opportunity to take the debate further, but the two contrasting worldviews were there for everybody to see. One worldview considers humanity as 'tourists' on this Earth, and the other considers humanity as 'pilgrims'.

There is a perennial wisdom which embraces the kind of simplicity that has been promoted by many great thinkers and visionaries. The current economic downturn and financial crisis offer us an opportunity to re-examine the culture of consumerism and the fashion industry, it is an opportunity to explore ways of living which offer contentment and creativity.

You are critical of our current money system, our desire to look good and acquire material possessions. Are you proposing a new kind of economics?

Yes, I am. I am proposing an economics of place rather than the current global casino economics. We can learn from the economy of nature. Let me give you an example:

There is a great yew tree in a churchyard in Dartington, Devon. Botanists believe that this yew is between 1,800 and 2,000 years old.

In other words almost as old as Christianity itself, and the tree was there long before the church!

"What is the secret of the sustainability of this great yew?" I asked Dartington's Head Gardener.

"The roots of this tree are as broadly and deeply embedded in the place as the branches are spread wide and high in the sky. Of course, you don't see the roots, but they take as much space as the trunk and the branches you can see," he replied.

"Is this true of most trees?"

"Yes it is. The great oak, the birch, the beech, the Lebanese cedar you see here in the garden are all embedded in their place. They have extensive networks of roots underground. If the trees did not have a sense of place, they would not survive."

What a perfect illustration of balance, harmony and wholeness – outward growth complemented by inward growth. If only the globalisers of the economy learned from the trees; if only the bankers, hedge fund holders, stock-market managers, financial experts and economists could see this relationship between inner growth and outer growth; if only manufacturers and retailers could realise that the economics of the planet has to be built on the economics of place. Economics without a sense of place has no place in economics. The breadth of the economy has to be in balance with its depth.

We cannot save the planet and destroy the place. We cannot serve the interests of the global community and undermine the interests of the local community. Large is lovely only if it is balanced by the beauty of the small; if we allow the small to diminish, then one day the large too will perish. We are facing a sorry state of affairs because the large banks have been allowed to swallow up the small saving banks and mutual societies; we sowed the seeds of the credit crunch when we abolished the credit unions; we laid the foundation of the economic downturn when we blindly pursued the path of unlimited economic growth. What goes up must come down.

So the economy has to stay within the parameters of ecology, ethics and equity. Day and night we chant the mantra of 'economy' while our ecology is in ruins, our ethics have been shelved and our principles of justice and equity are put on the back burner.

We blindly follow the religion of materialism, we worship the god of money, and we sacrifice everything at the altar of the economy. We indulge in consumerism as if there were no tomorrow. As a result, in the short term, banks are running out of money, consumers are short of cash, house prices are tumbling and unemployment is rising. In the longer term, we face global warming, global terrorism, global poverty and a population explosion.

The cause of all these multiple crises is our disconnection with the place to which we belong. Wherever we live, we need to be rooted in our place. If each and every one of us took care of our place, our home, our community, the soil by which we are sustained and the biosphere of which we are an integral part, then the whole planet would be taken care of. Being embedded in a place is a prerequisite for being free to look up at the sky and embrace the world. Love of place and love of planet are two sides of the same coin; when we belong to a place we belong to the planet. When we lose our place, we lose our planet.

It seems like you are advocating NIMBYism (saying that any development should be Not In My Back Yard)!

Yes I am, and I wish everyone would do the same. If every backyard is saved from motorways, airports, industrial estates, business parks and superstores, then the whole country and the whole world will be saved from them.

It amazes me to see that the great economists, industrialists, business leaders and politicians have even forgotten the true meaning of economy. They only think in terms of profit-maximisation and increased money supply whereas, as mentioned earlier, true economy means good housekeeping; proper management of all aspects of the home. The criterion of good house-management is to ensure that all the members of the household are living in harmony with each other and the place. And of course home is always a particular place. Money is only a means to a good economy, not the economy itself.

So in order to address the root causes of the economic downturn and the recession we face, we need to revisit the theory of economics itself, or the cycles of boom and bust will continue to infect our societies.

The present financial crash and market meltdown offers us an opportunity to look deeply and design a new paradigm of sustainability. The economics of debts and derivatives is fake and fragile. Bottom-up economics and trees and Terra Madre, or people and place, are resilient and reliable.

What booms can only bust; to avoid busts we also have to avoid booms.

The days lengthen as we approach the summer solstice, and we enjoy balmy summer mornings and warm evenings, but we cannot have long summer days for ever. After the solstice the days begin to shorten, and we have to accept the dark winter nights. Only near the Equator can we have days and nights in equilibrium. The challenge for politicians, economists and business leaders is to find an economic equator and a market equilibrium as a steady-state economy.

People talk about making poverty history, but to do that we also have to make wealth history. The very wealthy are the other side of very poor; high mountains are bound to create deep valleys. The culture of equilibrium requires balance, harmony, proportionality and a sense of place. Without them, we suffer boom and bust.

There are two roads to economic recovery. The first approach is to bail out the banks and fuel consumerism, to shore up the mortgage sector and hope to get back to business as usual. But the second option is to think holistically and invest in land and agriculture, in renewable energy and practical skills. The Earth is our true bank. We are at a crossroads – which path are we going to choose? The answer is obvious.

Let us celebrate our place and build the economy of place.

What is then the root cause of such individualism? Why do we feel separated, fragmented, and disconnected?

The universe is made of a balance between yin-yang forces, the forces of negative and positive, masculine and feminine, dark and light. When there is a balance between these apparently opposite forces, human societies flourish in a harmonious way. That is what happened with indigenous cultures. There was a balance between yin and yang. For them yin and yang were not opposites, they were complementary. But at certain times in history the human mind saw yang as superior to yin, masculine as superior to feminine, positive as superior to negative, light as superior to darkness, Heaven as superior to Earth. That view is the cause of our crisis. When we pursue one aspect of existence at the expense of the other, we upset the balance and harmony of our culture and of ourselves. When we pursue certain goals at the expense of balance, we end up dominating other people and nature. We also disturb our inner harmony. This is happening at this moment. We dedicate ourselves to certain goals such as attaining material wealth, financial prosperity and political influence, forgetting about mutual respect, mutual interest, and mutual harmony.

The cause of the crisis, which is manifesting in phenomena like global warming, global poverty, and global conflicts, is rooted in our mind itself. The solutions to global crisis are also rooted in our minds. When we are able to transform our mindset and cultivate a relational worldview, then we can return to a state of equilibrium.

How did ancient cultures manage to maintain such equilibrium?

Ancient cultures also had problems of desire, greed, anger, and attachment. But they cultivated a spirit of balance; they developed non-dualistic philosophies, such as advaita Vedanta, and Taoism. Metaphorically speaking, they cultivated the flowers – the bluebells, the primroses, the roses, the fragrant flowers; they discouraged the brambles and the poisonous plants, knowing that they cannot be completely removed, but at least reduce them, keep them under check. They did not water them, nor cultivate them. So a natural balance was achieved.

In the modern, industrial mindset we are confused. We think the poisonous plants are the flowers, and the flowers are just a superfluous decoration. So we have watered the seeds of anger, the seeds of control, of ego, of pride, of greed and of privilege. All these tendencies have been cultivated and encouraged. That leads to the idea of strong individualism. The ancient Indian and Chinese, the traditional Japanese and aboriginal cultures, American Indian and African cultures did not have the idea of a separate individual. The word 'individual' means 'indivisible'. In the same way as an individual is a self-contained entity, he or she is also indivisible from the family, the tribe, the human community, and also the Earth community. Everyone is part of the big picture. Now the meaning has changed, now 'individual' means 'separate being'. If we wish to live in a state of equilibrium, then we have to evolve into being members of our place and our planet.

So I would not blame any one culture for the crisis of our time. If the people of India and China are so pure and wise, why are they embracing this industrial mindset? It is easy for one group of people to put the blame on another group. For example, some Muslim fundamentalists put the blame on Western societies for the decadence and destruction of moral values. Similarly, some Western leaders have called countries like Iran "the axis of evil". Actually I don't like talking in terms of good and evil. It's too black and white. It's divisive. Rather than seeing the world as a place of struggle, conflict, competition, and contradiction, I prefer the term yin-yang, which means that all opposites complement each other. The yin-yang view of the world is to see opposites as counterbalancing, mutually enhancing, and interrelated. What we see as two are ultimately one.

The origin of personal crisis as well as global crisis lies in the idea of dualism. Wherever it is, whether it's in China, India, Japan, Africa or Europe, it is the belief in dualism, in separation, fragmentation and individualism that has misled us. The answer is not to turn away from Europe but to turn away from dualism and go back to relatedness. All beings are our kith and kin. The whole Earth is one family, one community.

There was a wonderful theologian in the United States called Thomas Berry, who sadly died recently. He said: "The universe is not a collection of objects, it is a communion of subjects." The whole of the universe is within me. If the rainforests are being cut down, my hair is being cut down; if the trees are being destroyed, my arms are being destroyed; if the rivers are being polluted, my bloodstream is being polluted. As E. M. Forster said, Only Connect!

How interesting that Thomas Berry, a Christian theologian and an American, refutes the implication of the ideas in Genesis that human beings have dominion over the Earth. Instead, Berry gives humankind a humble position within creation.

Many Christian mystics have shared the non-dualistic worldview, particularly the female Christian mystics such as Hildegard of Bingen and St Julian of Norwich. For them, the sacred and the divine are present everywhere. Ultimately there is no distinction between sacred and profane. God is not sitting somewhere beyond the sky. You don't have to look up to find heaven; heaven is here on Earth. God is present in the butterflies, in the worms, in the grass, in the flowers, and in the river; in every drop of water the divine is present.

Such a vision of the divine as present everywhere doesn't seem to recognise human frailty; and at the same time, the harsh reality of our age – full of conflict, violence, and cruelty – makes this vision seem like a dream.

Yes, it is like a dream, but why not dream? Why not have a vision of a more balanced and more harmonious future? But there is no such thing as utopia. Utopia means 'no place'. How can one live in a 'no place'? We have to be rooted in place, grounded in the realities of life. Of course there is good and there is bad, but sometimes the bad can be good and the good can be bad, so even this dualism does not really stand up. Good and bad are mixed together. Everything has a place, as long as it is in its place. Even a bit of anger has a place in appropriate measure. We put a little salt and a little chilli in our food, and that makes a good taste. If there were no salt and no chilli, then the food would be bland and would not taste delicious. Similarly a little bit of anger is OK. It is all a question of proportion. Everything has to be in the right proportion, in the right time, in the right place, in the right context and in the right proportionality. It is our consciousness which enables us to achieve this right balance of proportionality. When our consciousness is fully present, when we are mindful of our being, then even those emotions we call negative emotions will be accommodated in their right measure. This requires skilfulness, and these emotional, psychological, social and spiritual skills are developed through dedicated practice. But first, we have to dream!

These skills must grow from our hearts. Your mother wasn't trying to capture the world and put it into intellectual boxes – she was working with her heart; she was feeling and loving the environment through her heart. The heart is where the soul resides. The Egyptians, when they created their mummies, always put the heart back into the mummy. They threw away the brain and other organs, but they made absolutely sure that the heart would go back in, believing that the memory of the soul, resident in the heart, would be accessed through rebirth.

You are right to bring the heart into this conversation, because in the modern world of the intellect, the brain takes precedence and the heart is forgotten. The heart is the organ of feeling. When there is no feeling then there is no love, no compassion, no sense of relatedness. Most of the problems in the world are created by people who are highly educated and have well-developed brains but grossly underdeveloped hearts. Graduates, coming out of the great universities of the world such as Oxford, Cambridge, Harvard, the Sorbonne and others, are very smart and clever, but they mostly use their brains and very little heart.

With so much ingenuity they have developed nuclear power, nuclear weapons, and much other highly destructive weaponry. They have developed genetic engineering and genetically modified organisms, which undermine organic cultivation. They have developed methods of agriculture which put animals into factory farms, and the land is poisoned with chemicals and pesticides. They have developed technologies, from aeroplanes and cars to computers and mobile phones, which are resource-hungry, whose production and use cause pollution and have ultimately led to global warming. Brilliant economists have developed derivatives, hedge funds and umpteen other products which leave people in debt and the economy in crisis.

All these things have been developed because people were thinking only with their brains and not with their hearts. The so-called uneducated peasants of the world have played no part in producing nuclear bombs or instigating wars. They are not responsible for creating the technologies which lead to high carbon emissions or toxic pollutants.

Yes, that's true – one can hardly blame simple people like your mother for these global problems!

That's right, she would not even ride a camel or a horse to go to the farm, she would always walk. If someone suggested that she should take a ride on a camel, my mother would say, "How would you like it if the camel wanted to take a ride on you?!"

How long did it take her to walk to the fields?

About an hour each way. The farm was nearly three miles away from the house. My mother would always walk slowly. She enjoyed slow walks in nature, and this was a good and healthy thing. She would say that when you are walking, you perspire, and perspiration is good, it is like washing yourself from inside. Through sweating the body releases the poisons, and the body becomes clean from within as well as without. If you have not walked or not sweated, then you have not done your day's exercise. Mother would often ask me, *"Have you sweated today?"* This was her very commonsense 'peasant wisdom'. This two hours walking each day is comparable with the time people spend commuting to work in industrial societies. But the difference is that commuters driving their cars are sitting still doing no exercise, producing exhaust fumes which pollute the air, and feeling rather stressed. But we call it progress! My mother would be classified as a member of an underdeveloped society, whereas commuters in their cars would be classified as members of a developed society. Mother preferred pilgrimage to progress.

Your mother worked with the soil, whereas most of us in developed societies are disconnected from the soil. We don't know how to grow our food. Young people in our developed societies think that food comes from the supermarket. Many of them have never seen a farm.

Yes, my mother was a small farmer. Agriculture, for her, was as much a spiritual practice and a way of life as it was a source of food. She revered the soil because all life is dependent on the soil. While she cultivated the soil she also cultivated the soul. Giving tender, loving care to the land was a kind of meditation in practice. For her there was no distinction between living and meditating; she practised meditation as a way of life.

My mother saved her own seeds. There were no hybrid seeds in those days, never mind genetically modified seeds! My mother had never heard of chemical fertilisers or pesticides. Although she did not know of 'organic farming', she was naturally an organic farmer. For her, growing vegetables and crops and planting trees was a transformative experience. The process of growth from the seed to the plant is in itself a transformative process.

I remember her often talking about the seed of the banyan tree, which is the smallest seed that you can imagine; so small that if you put it in your hand, you may not even be able to see it. It's smaller than the mustard seed. You might have to use a magnifying glass to see it!

In Indian classic texts the banyan seed is often used as a metaphor, referring to the idea, similar to that of Blake, that the world can be found "in a grain of sand".

Once, Mother asked me to break a banyan seed;

"How can I break such a small seed?" I said,

"It is hardly possible, but try!"

When I finally crushed it, she asked,

"What do you see in it?"

"I see nothing."

"In this seed is the whole of that mighty banyan tree, which is one of the biggest trees in the world. It can have a thousand branches. If you go to see the famous, thousand-branch banyan tree in the botanical garden of Kolkata, you will not know which is the original trunk. It's so huge that it's almost like an enormous temple. All of that is inside this tiny seed. And you say you can't see anything!"

This is how she taught me the mystery and the majesty of the seed. What happens to the seed when it is planted in the soil? The seed goes into the soil and that particular seed will never return again. It's gone, it seems like its dead, but it's not dead – it's alive. It goes into the dark soil. It's in relationship with the soil, with the Earth, with the water, and with the sunshine. It remains there until one day a small plant sprouts. That small plant becomes a large tree, and the large tree has branches, has leaves, has fruit, and that seed, which died, is reincarnated into new seed. That one seed has given birth to thousands of new seeds – that's one kind of reincarnation – so the seed is a symbol of the continuity of life, the process of life. Interfering and messing about with this process of life is to show disrespect to life.

What is the meaning of the seed dying and reincarnating?

It means that death is not the end. Death and birth make up the cycle of life. The seed dying in the ground is giving birth to the tree. So death is valuable, death is important, death is as good as life. Death is as good as birth. Dying is as good as living. We live by dying. The moment we realise this, then we understand the cyclical nature of life. Much of our current thinking is linear: we think one is born, one lives, and then one dies, and that is the end of life. Therefore we are afraid of death. But death is not the end of life. My mother was never afraid of death. When she was 80 she said, "Now I choose to embrace death". So she went to her family, her daughters and sons, to her grandchildren and great grandchildren, to her friends and neighbours, to say goodbye. She said to them all, "I am frail, my faculties are failing, so from tomorrow I'm going to fast unto death." She fasted for 35 days, and died. She embraced her death, because for her death was a door into new life.

I've never heard of anything like that! Is that a normal practice in India?

It is an old Jain tradition. Some Hindus also practise it. My teacher, Vinoba Bhave became ill in his mid-seventies; he developed a severe case of ulcer in his stomach. He was taken to hospital, and the doctors said,

"We have to do a big operation and remove the ulcer from your stomach. You have to sign a disclaimer so that if something goes wrong, we are not responsible."

Vinoba asked,

"Is it really so serious that I need such a big operation?"

The doctors said that it was. So Vinoba said,

"I am in my mid-seventies, there's no need for me to live and go through all this trauma of such an operation. Let me go back home."

On the way back from the hospital he made a decision; he would stop eating, and would fast unto death. During that week of his fast, 30,000 people visited him. There were prayers, singing, religious chanting, mutual forgiveness, and great celebration of his life. The prime minister of India, Mrs Gandhi, came to pay her last respects. The news that Vinoba was fasting unto death spread all around India, and the day he actually died, 50,000 people came to take part in the funeral procession. Fasting in this way is a sacred tradition in India. Suicide is different, it is committed by someone who wants to escape their troubles and traumas, someone who is depressed and disappointed in life. Whereas this voluntary letting go of life is embracing death, welcoming death. It is love of life, and it is love of death.

Vinoba was your guru. He advised you to go around the world without money, and he died fasting. What kind of man was he?

Vinoba was a great friend and follower of Mahatma Gandhi, and for me he was a great mentor, and example of how to live. He lived like a pilgrim and died like a pilgrim. From an early age he took a vow of *brahmacharya*, celibacy. His two younger brothers also took the same vow. He devoted his entire life to the study of ancient texts of philosophy and religion. He was a Sanskrit scholar but also learned English, French, German, Japanese, Spanish, Arabic and a number of Indian languages. He translated the Koran and the New Testament into Hindi. He compiled essential Buddhist texts and Jain texts to make them accessible and available to the general reader.

After Mahatma Gandhi's death, he said,

"India has acquired political independence through non-violent means, but this independence is only the first step towards total independence, which means economic equity and cultural freedom."

Vinoba undertook a walking pilgrimage throughout India: for twenty years he was on the move, travelling north, south, east and west, covering 100,000 miles. I joined him in this pilgrimage.

Was there any specific purpose to this pilgrimage?

Essentially it was a spiritual pilgrimage. But, he undertook a mission of land reform. He calculated that if one-sixth of India's arable land was distributed among the landless poor, then they would have a secure means of livelihood. So he would go from village to village, meeting landowners and persuading them to give one-sixth of their land.

He would say,

"If you have five children, consider me your sixth child, a representative of the poor, and share one-sixth of your land with us."

This appeal, coming from a saintly, selfless pilgrim was so powerful that hundreds of thousands of landowners made a gift of land. All in all four million acres of land was given and distributed amongst the landless peasants. This was almost a miracle. In India land is so precious – and landowners are so attached to their land – that the giving of land in this manner is unheard of. This is an example of the power of the pilgrim's spirit.

Vinoba lived like a pilgrim and died like a pilgrim. We can learn from Vinoba's example, and not try to postpone the natural process of death. It is a pity that modern medicine tries to prolong life artificially, by this, that or the other means. Yet we need not fear death. I have said to my family that if I have a heart attack or any serious illness, please do not resuscitate me nor take me to the hospital. Do not call an ambulance, nor a doctor. If I am dying, let me die. There is nothing wrong in dying. We will all die, so let's die happily! Life and death are two sides of the same coin; there is no dualism.

That reminds me of Dōgen Zenji, who was the founder of the Sōtō sect of Zen Buddhism in the 13th century. Somebody asked him, "What is the Buddha?" He said, "The Buddha is life and death." That's a beautiful, simple answer. The Buddha is not just life, the Buddha is life and death. Buddha consciousness equals the consciousness of life and death.

A pilgrim has such a relationship with death. The attitude of a pilgrim is that all conditions, all situations, all encounters are there as a spiritual opportunity. There are no encounters, no hardships, no difficulties which should be wasted or discarded. All opportunities – negative or positive, comfortable or uncomfortable – present themselves as an opportunity for self-realisation, for self-purification and for the strengthening of the soul.

When something has weathered, in the English language we say that is has character. This old house in which we are sitting has character because it has weathered; it has gone through snow, wind, storms, rain, sunshine – every kind of weather. The building says, "Every weather is my opportunity. I'm not going to say that I only like sunshine and not snowstorms. All weather is good weather." That is how character is developed.

The pilgrim's mind is an open mind. A pilgrim also welcomes all weathers, all situations, all conditions with equanimity: pain or pleasure, gain or loss, victory or defeat, life or death. The pilgrim remains calm and steadfast throughout.

But in real life we have to try to seek success, to bring an end to suffering. How does the idea of yin-yang work in our business and in daily life?

As far as I have understood the teachings of the Buddha, who was perhaps the greatest teacher on the subject of suffering, the way to end suffering is to accept the suffering as part of life. Pain exists, and we cannot run away from it. Rough and smooth coexist, and we cannot have one without the other. Dark and light, left and right, success and failure go hand in hand. The state of enlightenment is reached when we are not perturbed by this so-called duality. In the big picture of external existence, all and everything has a place. William Blake said the same thing:

> It is right it should be so;
> Man was made for Joy and Woe;
> And when this we rightly know
> Through the world we safely go.

I'm beginning to get the flow of what you're saying. But I want to bring you down to the social and political reality of the world again. From most people's perspective, this situation of environmental

and economic crisis that we're in now is hopeless. There's no way that China or America is going to stop emitting CO_2. So where does your optimism come from? I think it's coming from the pilgrim spirit. You seem to be saying that even this terrible crisis is a learning opportunity. Even the fear of the destruction of civilisation, the collapse of the ecosphere, the disappearance of the bees, has something to teach us. These crises are like alarm bells to wake us up, to move ourselves towards transformation.

Towards transformation and also towards transcendence. We have a tendency and a desire to control; we think that we can control events, we can control the future, and that we can control our destiny. This tendency to control is a result of arrogance and ego. Rather than attempting to control events, we need to work to transform and to transcend; not get bogged down in problems but focus on solutions and rise above petty self-interest. The word 'crisis' in Chinese means danger and opportunity; the crisis we are talking about is an opportunity for transformation, for learning the limits of our powers, learning restraint, and learning to grow spiritually – in imagination, in poetry and in the arts – rather than just to grow economically or materially.

This crisis gives us the opportunity to see that all the so-called realists of the world – the smart scientists, the clever industrialists and cunning politicians – have brought us to the brink of disaster. They cannot save the planet. We need to develop a synthesis of realism and idealism. In fact, since we have given so much room to so-called realism, now it is time to give some extra room to idealism.

The realists don't seem to know how to solve the problems of war, of poverty, of hunger and deprivation; they don't know how to solve the problem of ecological and environmental destruction. They don't seem to know anything! They say that they are very clever, and that we should vote for them, we should leave our financial affairs and matters of security in their hands. We have done all this, but we have no security. There is no well-being. We are told over and over again that "money will make you happy, sophisticated weapons will bring security, and advanced technology will solve environmental problems." But the truth is that money is not going to make us happy. Weapons will not make us secure, and technology will not solve our problems.

For a hundred years we've tried to eliminate poverty, and yet it's increasing. For sixty years the United Nations has been trying to keep peace in the world, and yet there are so many unresolved conflicts, wars and genocides taking place. This stark reality gives us an opportunity to learn that we cannot control our destiny. We can only participate in the process of the universe with humility. We have failed to find solutions because all our efforts have been founded on the politics of self-interest and the politics of national interest. It is now evident that such politics is counterproductive. We have to design and devise policies and politics which go beyond self-interest, beyond national interest; politics and policies of mutual interest and mutual respect. President Obama is a flame of hope. In his inaugural address he used the words "mutual respect and mutual interest". Perhaps we are seeing the dawn of the age of transformation and transcendence.

The transformation we are seeking is from self-interest, communal interest and national interest to mutual interest. This can be achieved only by love. Love of the Earth, love of rivers, forests and trees, love of life, love of animals, love of each other; love is the real power. Unfortunately some environmentalists inculcate fear of doom and gloom and disaster. They advocate changes of policy to protect the planet, out of fear of the end of civilisation. But the force of fear is not good enough. We need to transcend our fears, and cultivate love. Love is a flowing fountain, never static and never the same. It is ever present, always fresh and always responsive.

Love is an overused word. It has lost its vigour and power. But it seems that for you the word 'love' is still potent and deeply meaningful.

Yes, you are right. People use the word love rather casually. If the word has lost its vigour and power, as you say, then I want to reinvigorate and re-empower it and restore the meaning which we take for granted.

Love rules supreme. Love diminishes separation. There is no 'I' or 'you'. There is only 'we'. Love acts like oil in the wheel of life; without love the wheel of life grinds and erodes. Life and all its activities are explicit, love is implicit, it is always there, or should be there. One need not be self-conscious of it, but when love is not there one can feel the pain. In love, not my will be done, but thy will be done.

In love there is mostly 'yes', and if there is 'no', then that 'no' is followed by 'yes'. Love is a listening device. Love is freedom from fear. When we trust in love and live in the house of love, then all goes well. Even difficulties become opportunities, problems become challenges, and a negative situation becomes a learning opportunity.

Love is a surrender of ego and a meltdown of pride. Love is a blossoming of beauty and a source of kindness. Love is the soul of all stories, an inspiration to all poetry. The greatest art is the art of love, for all other arts emerge out of the art of love. Life without love is empty and art without love is vanity. Love is all there is. Love is the solution to all our problems. Love is the answer to all our questions. Love is more than a thought or a concept or a principle, it is existence itself. Love *is*, therefore we are. Love is life imperative. I live in the landscape of love.

We are born of love. Our parents fell in love and from their love we came into being. All living beings are conceived in love. This is called the biology of love. Mother's love, father's love, love of our family and love of our friends make us who we are. The Earth loves us, the cosmos loves us. We too love the Earth and cosmos. The law of love is another name for the law of gravity.

Humans help each other because of love in their hearts. We give and we receive out of our love for each other. The love economy is greater than the money economy. The love economy brings equity and justice, whereas an economy based purely on money destroys social cohesion.

The politics of love brings peace. Politics without love leads to war. Love yourself, love your neighbours, love your friends, love your enemies. Love those who love you and love those who do not love you even more. The water of love will melt all anger. The fire of love will extinguish all hatred. Love will bring peace and prosperity, grace and gratitude, bliss and blessing. Let go of all your defences against love. Love is our true security and true defence.

Jesus loved and became Christ, and Gautama loved and became the Buddha. People say that the Buddha sat under a banyan tree, but really it was a tree of love which became known as the tree of enlightenment. Similarly, Gandhi loved and became the Mahatma, Teresa loved and became the Mother. We are transformed from ordinary to extraordinary through the alchemy of love. Sinners become saints through the transformative power of love.

Love is a potent potion to strengthen the soul and a nourishing nectar to sweeten the spirit. All is in love, and love is in all. Love is eternal and infinite. Love is god and god is love. I live and die for love's sake.

I invite you to visit me in the city of love. That is my only destination, the city of love.

But before I make my pilgrimage to the city of love I need to understand how to practise love in the forests of fear.

When we talk about love we have to understand what 'love' means. It means accepting every person and every situation as it is. When you say to somebody "I love you," it means "I accept you as you are." I don't love you because you are tall or short, wealthy or poor, educated or uneducated, black or white. I don't judge, I accept who you are and love you as you are.

When a pilgrim comes to a place or meets a person, there is no judgement. There is no liking or disliking, there is no rejection, there is no criticism. There is only acceptance. And out of this acceptance grows harmony. When you are in love with somebody you are in harmony with that person; when you are in love with a tree, you are in harmony with that tree. When you want to change that reality to suit your purpose, then that's a form of egocentric behaviour; that's the end of love and the beginning of attachment. When you want to change a person – or a situation, or the landscape, or the trees, or anything – to suit your design, your desire, your purpose, then that's the end of love.

Why do we have a state of anguish at this moment in the world? It is because we have lost a sense of love, a sense of acceptance, without judgement. We always want to design the world to suit us, we want to design nature for our benefit; that's not love, because it's a one-way street, while love exists in mutuality, in reciprocity, in acceptance, in appreciation.

When we don't appreciate things as they are and we want to change them, we end up losing the essence of the true nature of the other. Take, for example, dates: sometimes I go to a shop and buy dates, and when I come home and eat them I find that they are sugared! Can you imagine sugared dates? The date is one of the sweetest foods there is, and yet we seem to think they are not sweet enough, so we put sugar on them. If you love nature, then you want to buy dates as nature made them. As for me, I do not want them contaminated by any other substance! It is a kind of arrogance to think that we can improve on the original flavour of the date. Arrogance and love don't go together.

When we go to tribal peoples we think we love them, but then we want them to be schooled in Western-style schools, we want them to wear a suit and tie, or use Western medicines instead of their shamanic healing. What kind of love is that?

When I go as a pilgrim and meet Christians, I accept them; I meet Muslims and accept them; I meet rich and poor, communists and capitalists, blacks and whites, and I accept them all. I do not wish them to change in any way. Love is to love diversity, and diversity is not division. Love is to love unity, and unity is not uniformity. We are all one, and we are all different. Unity and diversity complement each other. It is wonderful that we have so many religions, cultures, languages and ways of living in the world. It is like being in a garden of a thousand flowers. If I was to come across a garden of only one kind of flower;

roses, red roses, in row after row, after a while I'd find it boring and monotonous. I want to be in a garden of roses, side by side with camellias, azaleas and lilies; that diversity in the unity of a garden is glorious. I even accept thorns with the roses, weeds with the flowers; that is what a garden is. To love a garden, you have to love all the plants as they are, in their place.

A heart without love turns to the head and wants to develop hybrid flowers, or genetically engineered flowers. I don't class that as love, I class that as manipulation. The way of the pilgrim is the way of acceptance, and the way of acceptance is the way of love.

Acceptance, and loving what is, is the only way to be at peace, to be happy with yourself and with the world. In nature there is a dark period, and there is a light period, and we accept them both. We have the season of winter, then we have the spring. We have the summer and then we have the autumn. We accept the changing seasons as they are, and we love them. The light and the dark, cold and warmth, blossoming, fruiting, falling and dying away – all are part of the process and the richness of existence. There is no need to fight the autumn and despise the winter; no need to defy the darkness and negate the nights. We see the brightest stars in the darkest nights. Let's love them all.

When you say love is god and god is love, that puts new meaning into the word 'god'. Like love, god is also an overused term. You have used it several times in our conversation. What does the word 'god' mean to you?

I will not be too worried if we have plenty of love in our hearts and no belief in a supernatural being called god. I live in the city of love rather than in the city of god. From the Jain perspective there is no creator god. In the Buddhist tradition, too, there is no concept of god. For the Hindus, god simply means pure consciousness; Brahma has no physical form.

How did we invent the idea of god?

Before the age of reason, before humanity invented science, before we created theories like gravity, relativity and evolution, and long before the idea of explaining existence only in terms of measurement, prophets, poets and philosophers all around the world were searching for a word, a principle, a concept, a truth which would embody all words, all concepts, all phenomena, all truths and all realities. They were looking for a word, knowingly or unknowingly, which would encompass the visible and the invisible, the tangible and the intangible, the physical and non-physical, material and non-material aspects of everything. They were seeking something which was universal, powerful and all-encompassing.

After a long search, a word was found, and it was god. Some called it Allah, others called it Brahma. Some called it Tao, others called it a Mystery or even Dreamtime. In essence, they all meant the same thing. They had discovered a way of making sense of the world.

Everyone rejoiced. They danced the dance of Shiva, they sang the ode to god. They praised the sun god, the rain god, the creator god, the destroyer god, the sustainer god, the personal god, the impersonal god, the one god and god of many gods. They also sang the praises of the Earth goddess and the goddess of wealth and wisdom. For some, god was a man with a long white beard in the sky pulling the strings and running the world. For others, god was not a person but an invisible sustaining principle. Whatever their belief, they built temples, shrines, sanctuaries, mosques and cathedrals in praise of gods and goddesses. They made pictures, frescos, tapestries and sculptures. They celebrated the known god and the unknown god through culture, creativity, imagination, rituals and festivities.

The idea of god became a source of joy and enchantment, but also dogma, delusion and quarrels. Fights broke out between my god and your god, true god and false god, one god and many gods. Seeing such a breakout of wars and disharmony, many thoughtful and rational people came to the conclusion that in order to bring peace and harmony among people they had to get rid of the idea of god itself, and find some other way of explaining the realities of existence.

Thus, the age of reason and science began. Now there was no room for magic or mystery, no room for myths or mysticism. The baby was thrown out with the bathwater. What could not be measured, quantified, analysed or replicated did not exist. Thus the world became polarised into believers and non-believers.

Whether we like it or not, the idea of god is with us and it will remain with us for a long time to come. I do not wish to spend my time debating or speculating the existence or non-existence of god. If you believe that god is a person then I part company with you, but I still love you, but if you believe that god is super-consciousness, then I am with you. Either way I love you. For me, love rules supreme.

Chapter Four

PILGRIM OF TRUTH

Who would true valour see,
Let him come hither;
One here will constant be
Come wind, come weather.
There's no discouragement
Shall make him once relent
His first avowed intent
To be a pilgrim.

Who so beset him round,
With dismal stories,
Do but themselves confound –
His strength the more is.

John Bunyan, *The Pilgrim's Progress.*

You come from a tradition where the politics of love has strong roots. You talked about your mother, you also talked about Vinoba; both of them represent the power of love and both of them were great pilgrims. Is there anyone else who has inspired you in a similar way?

Yes there is. Mahatma Gandhi was a great pilgrim of love. He did not go into politics to gain power for himself or for his party. In fact he said that if the British can rule over India through non-violent means, and make India their home, rather than using it as a source of wealth to be taken away to England, then he would be happy to have the British stay and rule. This was quite an incredible statement for a fighter for independence to make. Gandhi did not merely wish to replace white rulers with brown rulers, to exchange a foreign elite with a native elite. He wanted to transform India into a land where every single individual would have the opportunity for self-realisation, for achieving their true potential; a land where people and their natural environment are in tune with each other. Thus Gandhi embodied the politics of transcendence and the politics of process. He worked to bring about political, social and spiritual transformation.

What you are describing makes me think that the politics of process and transcendence require profound humility. Gandhi showed that humility is not self-denying or having low self-esteem. Humility is very powerful. Gandhi was a great symbol of the power of humility in the 20th century: a man who went to meet British leaders dressed in a *dhoti* (loincloth). He took on the whole British Empire and transformed it. This little guy in his *dhoti*, with some of his teeth missing, completely overwhelmed the British. His power was very different from the force of the British Empire. Gandhi had power, and the British had force.

Let us talk about transformation first. It's a word that many people use as if it was easy for anybody to transform themselves, but it's not easy because being humble is not easy. Without humility there is no transformation. In order for transformation to occur, we need to cultivate the power of humility, and release ourselves from the idea of using force. Power is from inside, from within. You are empowered by realising your inner power, whereas force is imposed from outside.

When I make this distinction between power and force, it is simply to differentiate the power of mercy, compassion and non-violence from the forceful attitude of domination, violence and exploitation. In other contexts the word force can be and has been used in a positive way, as William Blake spoke of "the force of the imagination" and Martin Luther King spoke of "soul force".

But for the purpose of our conversation, I prefer to use the word power to refer to the inner quality. Gandhi's power was the power of the soul – spiritual power – not the force of the gun, the police, the military, money, position, status or office. All these things are external. They grant the ability to impose and control through fear. What is outside you, what has been given to you, is force. What is inside you is power. The action of killing is force, because you are imposing your will on others; but to be prepared to die without fear, either in defence of your convictions, or to serve your fellow humans beings, or simply because death has come so you embrace it; this comes from inner power.

Speaking to Angulimala, the murderous bandit, the Buddha said: "I was a prince, and I would have been a king. I could have invaded others and become an emperor, but I thought that was futile. That's not power, it's only force. The real power is inside, and so I am in search of inner power, the real power, the true power, which is power and not force." In this way the Buddha was powerful, and 2,600 years later we remember him more fondly, admiringly, and with greater pleasure than thousands of emperors and kings who have come and gone, all of whom had force – but not power.

In *The Merchant of Venice*, when Shylock attempts to use the force of the law and demands a pound of flesh from his debtor Antonio, Portia, dressed as the lawyer, evokes the power of mercy, saying:

The quality of mercy is not strained,
It droppeth as the gentle rain from heaven
Upon the place beneath. It is twice blessed,
It blesseth him that gives and him that takes
'Tis mightiest in the mightiest, it becomes the throned monarch better than
* his crown,*
His sceptre shows the force of temporal power,
The attributes of awe and majesty, wherein doth sit the dread and fear of
* kings,*
But mercy is above this sceptred sway,
It is enthroned in the hearts of kings
It is an attribute of God himself . . .

Humility underpins the power of mercy and truth. That is why Mahatma Gandhi coined the word *satyagraha*, the power of truth or 'Truth Force'. Gandhi was able to show this power towards all people, including the British, and transform them through the power of truth. He said that the force of violence generates more violence: an eye for an eye leaves the whole world blind; there are no genuine military solutions to human conflicts, only the power of truth, love and mercy can resolve longstanding animosity and antagonism.

To exercise the power of truth and non-violence, *satyagraha*, the proponents chose not to inflict pain, suffering or hardship on their opponents, but rather to take the suffering upon themselves. They used the techniques of fasting, meditation and prayer to become strong in their resolve and purify their intentions, as well as influencing the hearts and minds of their opponents.

They prepared themselves to accept imprisonment as a consequence of challenging and breaking unjust laws. For example, when the British declared a tax on salt, Gandhi was shocked.

"The salt tax is a tax on the poor," said Gandhi, "because in a hot country like India salt is necessary, and everybody, including the poorest of the poor, need it."

So Gandhi marched to the sea, made salt, and broke the tax laws of the British government. Of course he was arrested. When he was brought to the courts he pleaded guilty and said to the magistrate,

"My lord, I am a lawyer, and I know that I have broken your law, because I believe it to be an unjust law. So please give me the harshest punishment you have in your books."

The magistrate replied, "Yes, Mr Gandhi, I am sorry to have to imprison you."

Gandhi replied, "My lord, don't be sorry, I will go to jail as a bridegroom goes to the wedding chamber."

The magistrate said, "I do hope that His Majesty's Government will find a way of releasing you before you have served the entire sentence."

Gandhi said, "There is no need for His Majesty's Government to release me from prison before my time is up. What I want is not the end of my hardship, I want His Majesty's Government to withdraw the unjust law first. Only then will I celebrate my release from prison."

Not only Gandhi but thousands of others joined the anti-salt-tax movement and incurred arrest. Eventually the salt tax was withdrawn. This is an example of *satyagraha* in action.

Yet Churchill called him a half-naked fakir!

That's right. When he came to London to negotiate independence for India with the British Government, he went to Buckingham Palace to meet the King. He wore only his loincloth and a shawl. He was half-naked! When he came out of Buckingham Palace there were lots of journalists there, and one from *The Times* asked him, "Mr Gandhi, how did you feel going to meet the King in Buckingham Palace in your loin-cloth? Didn't you feel a bit under-dressed?" Gandhi replied, "The King was wearing enough clothes for both of us!"

That was his humour and humility. He did not have to wear a tie, a suit and a hat to see the King, or for that matter to please Mr Churchill. He could go in his loincloth because he was a man of humility.

Gandhi was not only a man of humility, he was also a man of integrity.

Absolutely, there was integrity in his words and his actions. Sometimes people would say to him, "We have a conference, please give us a message. What is your message for our people?"

Gandhi would say, "I have no message to give. My life is my message."

Once Dr Lohia, a politician engaged in the independence movement, went to Gandhi, and said "Mr Gandhi, we have many great orators in the Congress party. We have great intellectuals and writers, like Nehru, like Patel, and others. But they don't have influence with the people like you do: when you give a call, hundreds of thousands of people follow you. They march, they fast, they spin the spinning-wheel, they get arrested and fill the jails, but only when you give the call. This does not happen when we ask people to do something. We give good speeches, but nobody listens. What is the magic, what is the trick, what is the secret of your power?"

Gandhi replied, "I don't know, but there is one thing I can tell you – I have never asked anyone to do anything that I have not done myself, and tried in my own life."

That is the power of integrity. His words, his actions and his life were one integral whole.

Once a woman came to Gandhi with her son and said, "Mr Gandhi, my son eats too many sweets. Please tell him that sugar is very bad for his teeth. He won't listen to me, because I am his mother; but if you tell him, he will listen to you."

Gandhi was a bit reluctant. He fell silent for a few minutes. Then he said: "Dear mother, come back in a fortnight, and I will speak to your son."

She left, and two weeks passed. Then the woman came back with her son and said, "You asked to me come after two weeks, so here I am. My son is still eating too many sweets, and he will not listen to me. Please speak with him."

So Gandhi said to the boy: "You know too many sweets are not only bad for your teeth, they are not good for your whole body. Now you are young and do not see the consequences of eating badly, but later you will come to regret it, when you lose your teeth or get fat."

The boy went out to play. The mother was a bit puzzled, so she asked Gandhi, "Why did you wait two weeks to tell my son this? You could have given the same advice when we came last time."

Gandhi said, "Mother, at that time I myself took a bit of sugar in my milk, so how could I ask your son to do something which I was not doing myself? But in the last two weeks I also decided to give up taking sugar." That is integrity. Gandhi said: "Be the change you wish to see in the world."

Gandhi was often hard on himself. Was it really necessary to be so extreme?

The path of transformation is not for the faint-hearted! The way of the pilgrim has many hardships. For Gandhi, restraint was as important as humility and integrity. Without restraint we are wasteful, careless, and indifferent in our relationship with the material world. There is a well-known anecdote illustrating his restraint.

Once Gandhi was staying with his friend Jawaharlal Nehru, who later became the first prime minister of independent India. In those days, there was no running water in Nehru's house. In the morning people used a jug of water to wash. Accordingly Nehru brought a jugful of water for Gandhi to wash his face, his teeth, and his hands. Nehru was looking after his treasured guest himself. As Gandhi was washing his face, and Nehru was pouring the water, they were also talking; they were talking about the politics of India, how to get rid of the British, how to organise the next phase of the independence movement. They were talking intensely. Suddenly the jug of water was empty.

Nehru said, "Please wait a minute; I will go and fetch another jug of water."

Gandhi replied, "What? Another jug of water! Have I finished that whole jugful of water without completing my wash?"

Nehru could not understand, he was puzzled and he said, "Why are you so worried about a jug of water? Don't worry, Gandhi, I'll get more water, there is no shortage of water in my town. There are three great rivers – the Ganga, Jamuna and Saraswati – flowing though my city. There is no problem; you are not in the desert of Gujarat, your home state, you are in the fertile land of Allahabad,"

Nehru saw that Gandhi was in tears. Nehru was even more surprised at Gandhi's reaction, when Gandhi said, "You may have three rivers flowing through your city, but my share in those three rivers is only one jug of water each day. I have been very wasteful today, I have used too much water. Whether I am in a desert or in your fertile land, I should take only a little water."

That is Gandhi's restraint, and I agree that restraint is one of the essential qualities of a pilgrim. But there was much more to Gandhi than his humility, integrity and restraint. Can you tell me more about his life and his main ideas?

He was born as Mohandas Karamchand Gandhi on 2nd October 1869 in the town of Porbandar in Gujarat in western India. His father, a devout Hindu, was prime minister in his native princely state. The young Gandhi was sent to England to study law. Then he went to South Africa to practise it. There he was thrown out of a segregated train on the ground of his colour. Shaken by this unjust encounter, Gandhi mounted a campaign of non-violent civil disobedience to expose the evils of apartheid. Inspired by the writings and example of Henry David Thoreau, Gandhi stirred the political circles of South Africa. Faced with the brute force of weapons and prisons, Gandhi used the power of non-violence and truth, and proved its superiority. Surprised by the use of this technique, the perpetrators of apartheid found themselves confused and powerless. Thus the seeds of freedom from apartheid were sown in South Africa.

What did Gandhi do after his work in South Africa?

He returned to India and refined his techniques of *satyagraha* (see page 92) and introduced it to the people of India to empower them to wage their struggle for freedom from colonialism. His movement became so powerful and effective that Britain could not withstand it, and eventually agreed to grant independence to India.

While the struggle was in progress, Gandhi was working on ideas for a new social order for a truly free post-colonial India. These were to form a new 'trinity' of ideas. The first was *sarvodaya*, the 'Upliftment of All'. The Western system of governance is based on the rule of the majority, so-called democracy. This was not good enough for Gandhi. He wanted no division between the majority and the minority. He wanted to serve the interests of each and every person. Democracy is also limited to caring for the interests of human beings. Democracy working with capitalism favours the few who have capital. Democracy together with socialism favours the majority, but is still limited to humans. *Sarvodaya* includes the care of the Earth; of animals, forests, rivers and land as well as people. For Gandhi life was sacred, and so he advocated reverence for all life, for humans as well as other-than-humans.

The second aspect of the Gandhian trinity is *swaraj*, 'Self-Government'. *Swaraj* works to bring about a social transformation through small-scale, decentralised and participatory structures of government; and *swaraj* also implies self-transformation, self-discipline and self-restraint on a personal level. A moral, ethical, ecological and spiritual foundation in the personal, social and political sphere is necessary to build good governance.

The third part of the trinity is *swadeshi*, 'Local Economy'. Gandhi opposed mass-production, and favoured production by the masses. For him, work was as much a spiritual necessity as it was economic, so he insisted on the principle that every member of society should be engaged in manual work. He believed that manufacturing in small workshops and cultivation of the arts and crafts feed the body as well as the soul; and that the long-distance transportation of goods, competitive trading and relentless economic growth would destroy the fabric of human communities as well as the integrity of the natural world.

Gandhi was a great champion of Hindu-Muslim solidarity – this was appreciated neither by the fundamentalist Hindus nor by the fundamentalist Muslims. Against the wishes of Gandhi, India was partitioned on religious lines, and hundreds of thousands of Hindus and Muslims were massacred or made refugees. One Hindu fundamentalist, Nathuram Godse, assassinated Gandhi on 30th January 1948, just six months after India's independence. As a consequence, Gandhi lost the opportunity to continue his work for a new social order, and his trinity had only a limited impact.

Chapter Five

PILGRIM'S MIND

Good thoughts his only friends,
His wealth a well-spent age
The earth his sober inn
And quiet pilgrimage

Thomas Campion, *A Book of Airs XVIII*

There is a fear that giving up the consumer lifestyle we have grown accustomed to will lead to hardship. We worry that without this abundance of industrial products we will have a life of suffering, as if we were exchanging a silk garment for a hair shirt – or Gandhi's loincloth! When we think of an environmentally sound lifestyle, we think that it is going to be limiting; it's going to be a drag.

What I am proposing is the exact opposite of what you are worried about. I am talking about an elegant, simple, beautiful, exciting, creative, colourful, healthy and wonderful way of living. It will be much more fun! At the moment people are too busy to enjoy their lives. They have lost the luxury of time. Their busy lives are very stressful. Commuting from suburbia to the city, working from morning to evening in factories, shops and offices, the joy of life has been squeezed out. People in industrial societies like Japan, the United States and Europe, and in big cities like Mumbai, Kolkata, Delhi and Mexico City – they all have no time. They are time-poor, time-starved, time-hungry. When I was growing up, people used to say, "When the gods made time, they made plenty of it. What is the hurry?" So why can we not create a future which is time-rich? Why not slow down and go further? Why not do less, and do it well? Why not have less quantity but more quality?

People have also lost the luxury of good food. Having fresh, healthy, delicious, organic food from your garden is one of the greatest pleasures that people in modern times are missing out on. When we get food wrapped up in plastic, imported from somewhere far away – things like apples, oranges, or bananas which have been harvested unripe, and then ripened in artificial conditions – the taste and flavour of the food have been squeezed out. There is no celebration of food. Don't you look forward to enjoying more fresh and delicious food on the table, with a lot of time to share it with your friends and family?

Aren't you encouraged that your food will be grown compassionately, non-violently and organically? That it will be free of chemicals, fertilisers and pesticides? That agriculture will involve caring for the land and for animals? That people who work on the land will not have to breathe pesticides and plough hundreds of acres on a solitary tractor? Instead of monocrops you will have hundreds of varieties of rice, of wheat, of apples, of potatoes, each with its own distinctive flavour, and each suited to its own particular climate. Should we not aspire to have such biodiversity and cultural diversity in food?

But the food in modern times is so convenient – we go to supermarkets and get everything from around the world in one place.

But at what cost to us, to our families and our environment? We live in the world of TV dinners, junk food and ready meals. This is the world of mass-produced, highly packaged and thoroughly commercialised food systems created by the supermarkets and agribusiness. This is the world where the knowledge and skills of growing food are disappearing, where the art of cooking is being lost, and where the delights of dining together are diminished. We have lost control of the sources of food. Most of us have no say in how food is grown, how it is distributed, how it is priced or even how it is cooked.

Access to food should be a fundamental human right, for food is nature's gift to all. Feeding people and all living creatures is intrinsic to life, to existence, but sadly food has become a commercial commodity. The primary objective of those who are in the food business is to make money; feeding people has become secondary. No wonder that we face multiple crises such as the rising cost of food, an obesity epidemic, malnutrition and world hunger.

An urgent challenge facing us all is to look at the first principle of food systems, which is to sustain life. The primary responsibility of governments and business leaders is to develop policies and practices which can meet the food needs of all people around the world, while at the same time protecting the integrity and sustainability of the Earth itself.

Growing, cooking and eating good food is an ecological imperative. But food is more than just fuel for the body: it is a source of spiritual, social, cultural and physical nourishment.

Earlier you asked me, "What can we do to combat global warming, environmental degradation, social injustice, the breakdown of families and communities? Where do we start if we want to address these big issues?" My answer is: Let us start with food. Let us eat local, organic, seasonal and delicious food. Let us take control of food into our own hands, rather than leaving it in the hands of the big producers and distributors.

The intimate action of eating the right food – and good food – is a solution to the ultimate problems of global warming and global hunger. Food is a microcosm of the macrocosm. When we focus on food, we immediately pay attention to the multinational corporations who turn food into a commodity; to the genetic engineering of seeds, where crop control and agricultural decisions pass from peasants and farmers to managers and engineers. If we are concerned about industrial-scale farming, factory farming, food miles, soil erosion, cruelty to animals, fast foods, fatty foods and junk foods, then we have to start with a look at our plate and what is on it. The food in our pantry and in our kitchen is ultimately connected to global warming and global poverty, as well as to our health.

Our focus on food will lead to land reform, self-sufficiency, farmers' markets, allotment gardens, slow food, artisanal food, permaculture, agroforestry and much more. We have to transform our personal relationship with food; that is the first step towards transforming political, economic and social policies on food. Personal and political are two sides of the same coin; we cannot do one without the other. We start with the personal, and stride toward the political; then there is integrity in what we say and what we do. Of course we cannot stop at just personal lifestyle change; we need to communicate, organise and build a popular movement to put pressure on governments and businesses to change their ways.

Are you prepared to put your hands in the soil? Have you time to bake bread and share your meals with your family and friends? If you have no time to cook and eat properly, then you have no time to live. As Molière said, "It is good food not fine words that keeps me alive."

I appreciate and admire your passion and enthusiasm. But are you not being a bit romantic? I am still worried that people will find it difficult to relinquish their convenient lifestyles.

This is understandable. We have been conditioned, we have become habituated. It is difficult to imagine anything different. But I advise you, my friend, leave your worries behind and embrace a life which is authentic. Nowadays we are inundated with lots of products, over-whelmed by choice – but is our society enjoying well-being? We have had sixty years of plenty, and yet the feeling of insecurity is on the rise, anxiety and depression are prevalent.

We are being sold a system that looks glamorous, glittering, and ostentatious. There's an external show, but the real substance is miss-ing. And that's why a new vision of society is emerging: it is a vision of joy and quality, with high-quality food, high-quality clothes and high-quality houses. At the moment, our industrial system is based on con-sumerism and mass production, so it has to foist mass consumption upon us. More, more, more! Whereas the emergent vision is replacing 'more' with 'better'. Less is more. Have less food, but delicious, high-quality food, then you will feel more satisfied and you will be health-ier. Have fewer clothes, but beautifully made clothes, and you will be more comfortable. Have a smaller house, but let it be well-crafted and personalised, and you will feel more at home.

We have been sold a fantasy that one day work will be abolished. All activities, production and services will be done by machines. But this is a mirage. In spite of a plethora of machinery in industrial societies like Europe and America, people work harder than ever. But the reality is that rather than the machines serving people, people have become servants of machines. This work is soul-destroying because, rather than people serving people, people are serving machines. We have to wake up from this fantasy and come back to Earth, come back to reality: the reality is that there can be no human existence without engaging ourselves in physical activity.

Work is natural; we do not need to escape from work. The fear of hardship is partly a fear of work. But right work is not hardship. Work is not drudgery, work is not labour, work is worship. Work is dignified. Let's restore the dignity of work. Work is pleasure when it is done in the right way, with the right motivation. When the Japanese potter Shoji Hamada was making pots, it was not drudgery; for British potter Bernard Leach making pots was not drudgery, it was a joy and pleasure. When somebody is building a beautiful house, it's not drudgery – it is an authentic expression of creativity and imagination. It is not only the poor who should work while the rich can just sit and enjoy Coca Cola. Everybody should have the opportunity to express themselves through their work. Work is an art; all work can be a work of art if it is done well. Whether it be gardening, building a house, making clothes, making pots, making chairs, they should all be products of the arts and crafts. Teaching in a school, working in a hospital, designing a book, running an organisation – all these can all be works of art if they are skilful, if they enhance relationships and friendships, if they fire imagination, if they bring joy and satisfaction. To paraphrase Ananda Coomaraswamy, art is not a special kind of work, but all work is a special kind of art.

So freedom from the fantasy of idleness will free us from the fear of hardship and hair shirts!

What you are talking about is a pilgrim's attitude to work. But in common parlance the word 'pilgrim' evokes something other-worldly, far from the world of work.

But remember: I'm an Earth pilgrim. My concern is not the other world but this world, this Earth. When I live and act in the spirit of a pilgrim, then whatever I do is transformed into being part of the pilgrim's journey. I am not seeking heaven, or salvation, or some kind of idealised next life: I am seeking a deep commitment to life in the here and now, upon this Earth, in this world. The Earth is a sacred temple. It's a place where we find our liberation, we find our enlightenment, we find our self-realisation. This is the place where Buddha, Jesus Christ, Mohammad, Lao Tsu, Mahatma Gandhi, Mother Teresa and St Francis found their self-realisation. This is the place where Shakespeare, Beethoven, Bach, Tolstoy, Kalidas, Bashō and countless others found their fulfilment. No need to be other-worldly! This is the place where we become pilgrims, through work, through living, through engaging. Engagement is not attachment. Engagement is to realise that we are all entangled and connected, and through that connectivity we become pilgrims. There is nothing else that we need to do to become pilgrims. We don't have to go for training, we don't have to go to university, we don't have to read books; the moment we realise that we are pilgrims we become pilgrims. That's all there is. It's as simple as that.

All right, it's not other-worldly. But when people use the word pilgrim, they relate it to the idea of travelling with a spiritual purpose and leaving behind the hustle and bustle of daily life. But you don't seem to mean that.

Being a pilgrim is a state of mind; it has nothing to do with actual travel. Travelling is symbolic. We travel in life, and through life. All of life is a journey. The journey is metaphorical as well as literal. Making a journey from A to B is only the ostensible goal. But going from A to B is not the point of the pilgrimage. Wherever you are, with your consciousness, with your way of being, with your way of looking at the world, with your way of connecting with the world, you are a pilgrim. A pilgrim is someone who sees life as a sacred journey, who sees the Earth as a sacred home, who sees the universe as a process.

When you are making a physical journey and living thanks to the hospitality of people along the route, you experience the generosity of your host and humility in yourself. That experience can linger even after the physical journey. So, the physical pilgrimage and the metaphorical pilgrimage are interrelated. We make the outer journey in order to make an inner journey. Our inner landscape is shaped by the outer landscape and vice versa. Therefore, by making a journey to holy places, such as the River Ganges, Mount Kailash, Santiago de Compostela or Iona, I was moved to explore my inner landscape, and make my journey to the holy source within. The abundance and the majesty of the Earth inspires me and lifts my spirits. Thus, the outer journey and the inner journey become one.

Nomadic societies, such as the Maasai in Africa, are always moving in the outer world. All human societies were nomadic at one time. Now most of us have become settled, in a place. Yet, in the spirit of pilgrimage, we can maintain our nomadic mind, which is a detached mind. As nomads are unbound by place and are continuously fresh in their experiences, pilgrims, with their nomadic minds, are free from the bondage of desires and maintain their innocence of heart. However, in order to touch the nomadic mind we undertake outer journeys from time to time. Going on a physical pilgrimage is no mere ritual, it is a meaningful way of expanding our minds. Climbing a sacred mountain, being immersed in a sacred river, gazing at the sacred stars, losing ourselves in the sacred desert, our consciousness extends beyond the beyond. Then we realise that the world is not a static, stagnant reality; it is a moving feast!

If you only want to get somewhere, then you are a tourist. A tourist looks for self-gratification. A pilgrim seeks to commune with the other and unite with the whole. For a pilgrim, every moment is a sacred moment, a beautiful moment; every moment is an opportunity to connect. Connecting and relating is true spirituality. Spirituality is present everywhere, in every moment, at every time. Just as there is no moment when we are not breathing, in the same way there is no moment when we are not spiritual. Spirituality is like breathing; without breathing we cannot survive. The root of the Latin verb *spirare* gives us the words 'inspire' and 'expire'. To breathe in is to inspire, when we stop breathing we have expired! No wonder that the classic form of meditation is to pay attention to breathing. If someone says "I am not spiritual," I ask, "Are you not breathing?" Of course, spirit requires matter. To breathe you need nostrils, you need a mouth, you need your skin – you need matter to breathe. Matter is a vehicle for the spirit.

When you speak about expanding consciousness and extending the mind by letting the inner landscape connect with the outer landscape, it sounds wonderful. Can you maintain such exuberance throughout the physical journey? And also in your life?

That would be latching on to one-dimensional reality. Life is not like that. Nor is pilgrimage like that. As a pilgrim I experience despondency, doubt, ambivalence, fear and uncertainty. I have gone through times when I felt infinite loneliness. These are very important moments in a pilgrim's life. I had to go though such a 'dark night of the soul'. Without going through difficulties, without going to the bottom of the valley, and getting lost in its dark ravines, you do not gain strength. Pilgrimage does not mean that all is smooth and simple, that all is good and well organised. When I was in a situation where I did not get food, I felt resentment. "Why are people not hospitable to a pilgrim?" Yet, that was the god-given opportunity for me to fast. When I did not get any shelter, then again I would feel vulnerable and complain about the lack of generosity, thinking "Why did I come on this god-forsaken journey? I could have stayed at home in comfort, in the clean sheets of my bed, and beside the warm fire of my living-room." Yet that was again my opportunity: to sleep under the stars and connect with the whole universe, with the cosmos. These moments came to tempt me to give up my journey, but such moments of despondency and despair also pass. For this reason, undertaking a physical journey is necessary because you come face to face with your fears and you discover that the fear you were gripped by was momentary and illusory.

As I pass through air and space, fears pass through my mind, every-thing passes.

But we are conditioned to have fears from a very early age. Our par-ents and our teachers sow the seed of fear in us.

Many of the problems we have in our families stem from fear. Parents are attached to their children, they want to protect them; they them-selves are frightened of the children having accidents, or not succeed-ing at school, or not getting a job or not finding a partner. Children pick up on those fears, so they grow up full of fear, and pass those fears on to their children, and so it continues. We can break this chain only by developing a pilgrim's mind. Then we can allow our children to grow freely, allow them to follow their own path, allow them to be themselves, rather than be copies of their parents.

Children react and rebel against parents because they don't want to be copies of their parents. Many, many struggles and conflicts between parents and young people are due to this very unfortunate and negative state of affairs. Parents feel as if the children are their possessions. They want children to behave in a particular way, which is impossible because children come with their own destiny, their own attitudes, and their own aspirations. The pilgrim attitude is to see that the child is a gift. As parents we must nurture children, as Khalil Gibran said:

> *Your children are not your children . . .*
> *They come through you but not from you . . .*
> *You may give them your love but not your thoughts,*
> *For they have their own thoughts*
> *You may house their bodies but not their souls,*
> *For their souls dwell in the house of tomorrow, which*
> *You cannot visit, not even in your dreams.*

If we were to follow Gibran, we would break the chain of fear and then children would grow up to be bold and free from fear.

A child is already a complete being and not an underdeveloped adult. When the child has inspiration from within, that inspiration should be followed. If we try to control the child, if we manipulate the child, then we are moulding the child according to our image, and not accepting the child as she or he is. This is where fear begins.

In the Christian tradition they say you have to become like a little child in order to reach the kingdom of heaven. Similarly in the Zen tradition the child's mind is considered to be the mind of innocence, the mind of purity. The Zen master Shunryu Suzuki wrote a book called *Zen Mind, Beginner's Mind.*

Exactly. Zen masters teach us to return to beginner's mind, child's mind, but we the adults want our children to acquire adult's mind! A clever mind, an anxious mind, a mind full of plans, ambitions, and desires. Such a mind is difficult to silence. The stillness of meditation and busyness of the adult mind are incompatible. That is why Zen masters want us to develop beginner's mind, a calm mind, a contemplative mind.

Dōgen said "You don't meditate to become enlightened; you meditate because you're already enlightened."

Yes, the child's mind is already innocent and enlightened. If we, the adults, can aspire to develop a childlike clarity and concentration, we will be enlightened and we will be able to meditate.

The word 'Zen' comes from the Sanskrit word 'dhyāna', which means 'meditation'. 'Dhyāna' became 'jhāna' in south-east Asia, then it became 'Chán' in China, and then it became 'Zen' by the time it reached Japan; so basically 'Zen' means 'meditation'. What is meditation, other than being childlike, being innocent, being present, mindful, aware, attentive; and to live in the moment. If you are 100% present, like a child, in whatever you are doing, if you give total attention and live in mindfulness, then you are in meditation. Meditation is not just closing your eyes and sitting cross-legged. That is good practice and a good start, a step in the right direction. Like you practise music to master the art, you sit cross-legged to master your mindfulness. You need to learn some techniques. So it's a good thing to sit and close your eyes, sit cross-legged, keeping your body straight and to be aware of your breathing, but that is not the whole story – it is just the tip of the iceberg. The real big iceberg is underneath, that iceberg is to be able to live consciously every moment of your life. You transform the day into a time when you are totally attentive, present, mindful and aware. Whatever you do, you do with awareness. Then you are in cooking meditation, gardening meditation, walking meditation, even sleeping meditation. A pilgrim lives a life of meditation.

Every word you speak becomes meditation if you speak with awareness. Then you can know what effect your words will have on the listener; will your words inspire confidence, or will they agitate the listener? You are aware of the consequences of your words, the results of your words. If you are aware of all that, then even your conversation becomes a speaking meditation. The language of the pilgrim is to speak the truth but say it sweetly. Develop the skill and the technique of speaking without using abrasive or offensive words.

Every breath becomes meditation if you breathe with awareness. When you breathe in, you know "I am breathing in," and when you breathe out, you know "I am breathing out," you know the sensation of your breathing, you know the pace of your breathing, and then you are in breathing meditation. So meditation in Zen is a way of life; it is not just sitting cross-legged and with the eyes closed, but it is how you live that is meditation.

Some meditators claim that they can levitate physically during meditation. Is that possible?

Everything is possible! I will not doubt or deny any possibility. However, I myself have not seen anyone levitating! For me, as a pilgrim, levitation is not a literal idea, it is a metaphor. For me it is not important to levitate physically and rise about the ground bodily. I wish to levitate spiritually, to rise above the gravity of greed and fear, to transcend all my desires, destinies and destinations. The focus of Jain meditation is on inner levitation!

You were brought up as a Jain monk, which is somewhat similar to Zen. Do the Jains also give similar importance to meditation?

Yes they do. As a monk I learned to practise two hours of meditation every morning and two hours every evening. To meditate is to still your body, to pay attention, to be aware. Of course, in the still body the movement of the mind and the movement of the breath continue. So I learned to connect those two movements by focusing the mind on the breath. I was taught to be aware that the breath I am taking is the same breath of life which sustains all human beings, all animal beings, all plant beings, all life in the oceans and rivers. Thus all life is connected. The air I breathe knows no borders, no barriers, no walls. The air I breathe permeates throughout the universe. The air I breathe touches the stars, the moon, the sun, the galaxies, the planets. Thus when breathing I am connected with the whole Earth, with the whole universe, and with all the other universes that I may not know. The air I breathe has existed since the beginning of time, so through the air I am connected to all of the past, and all of the future into eternity.

How wonderful! Apart from attention on breathing, what else did you focus on?

In the first part of the two-hour meditation I would only pay attention to breathing. Then in the second part I would contemplate kindness, compassion, truth, love, reverence, and above all non-violence.

The Jain tradition is very keenly committed to the principle of non-violence. For Jains, non-violence to oneself comes first. Quite often we are very violent to ourselves, and if we are violent to ourselves we cannot be non-violent to others. So being non-violent to yourself is the first step. By meditating on non-violence you learn to be kind to yourself, kind to your body, kind to your mind. Even when you are being violent to others, in effect you are being violent to yourself. When you speak harsh words to others, you are being harsh to yourself, because your harsh words will impact on your own well-being; your own equanimity and equilibrium will be upset.

When you are non-violent to yourself, non-violence will radiate from you. If you love yourself, then love will radiate from you; when you are compassionate to yourself, you will radiate compassion; for we are full of compassion, love, and non-violence.

When you are non-violent to yourself, then it is easy to be non-violent to your fellow human beings. During meditation I would reflect on how to practise non-violence through serving and helping my fellow human beings. There is no greater act of *dharma*, righteousness, than being of service to someone who is in need of help, and there is no greater sin than the sin of inflicting suffering on others. For when I relieve the suffering of others, my sense of ego, pride and separateness melts away. And when I inflict suffering on others I am binding myself in the knots of separation and in the chains of ego. A Jain monk is called *nirgranth*, which means, without knots, without bondage. So day after day I learned to meditate on being *nirgranth*. In my meditation I would also contemplate being non-violent not only to humans but also to beings other-than-human: non-violent to bees, birds, wasps, worms, cows, cats, dogs, trees, rivers and even mosquitoes.

Practising non-violence leads to kindness, and when you are kind to others, you are happy.

This seems to be self-evident, yet why is it that people are cruel to each other? Surely cruelty is the cause of one's own unhappiness, yet we deliberately engage in cruelty.

Cruelty is the consequence of egocentric habits. When I am seeking *my* happiness, I am separating myself and becoming ego-centred. Conversely, when I am seeking *your* happiness I am relating to you, and thus becoming eco-centric. There's a great deal of difference between 'ego-centred' and 'eco-centred' behaviour. 'Eco-centred' behaviour is centred in relationships, and 'ego-centred' behaviour is centred in isolation. This is a paradox, for when I seek happiness for myself, I lose happiness; when I seek your happiness, I gain happiness; when I am kind to you, I am happy. The fundamental principle of non-violence is to do no harm to others if you wish to be happy; the moment you harm others, you will be miserable – because you and the other are not separate. The other is none other than you.

There is no Muslim world, there is no Christian world, there is no communist world, there is no capitalist world, there is no white world, there is no black world; there is only one human world. The Buddha did not desire just his own liberation; he said that he did not want to be liberated until all sentient beings are liberated. He would wish to return to the Earth, birth after birth, and be kind to all sentient beings. That is the reason behind the tradition of the Dalai Lamas. They are the Buddha reincarnate. In other words, do not seek self-salvation, seek the salvation of all, which includes you!

How do you express this non-violence towards others?

You do it through gratitude. As a monk I walked barefoot and with a begging bowl. If someone gave me food, I expressed my gratitude. If someone didn't give me food, even then I expressed gratitude: "If you don't give me food, I am grateful to you that you are teaching me how to be equanimous, how to keep my temper, how to remain calm and compassionate even in adverse situations. You are my teacher; by denying me that piece of bread you are teaching me patience and equanimity. I am grateful to you."

This sense of gratitude is fundamental to a Jain pilgrim. The path of the pilgrim is a path of gratitude at all times; gratitude not only when things are done that you can readily appreciate, but at all times. The moment you have gratitude, you have expressed your non-violence towards others.

The word gratitude means gracious attitude. It is easy to be gracious to those who are gracious to you. But a pilgrim is gracious all the time, regardless of whether others are gracious or not. This is true gratitude.

People are so often gracious to us, yet we take them for granted, and forget to be grateful. Workers build houses, manufacture shoes, design clothes, ship goods, yet when do we express our gratitude to them? We think that if we have paid them a few coins in return, that is the end of the story. The trees give us fruit, shade, wood, fragrance, but do we express gratitude to them? The river quenches our thirst, refreshes our bodies, irrigates our land, but do we ever thank her? The Earth is our gracious host. Are we her gracious guests? A pilgrim is ever grateful.

After all that Jain meditation, the practice of non-violence and gratitude, you left the Jain order. Why?

Because I happened to read the autobiography of Mahatma Gandhi; if there was ever a book which changed my life, this was it. Talking about those on a spiritual path, Gandhi said that spirituality is not outside the world, it is in the world. Instead of a few people leaving the world, seeing it as a trap and wanting to liberate themselves from it, we should transform the world. What is the good of going and living in a monastery to practise truth, non-violence and spirituality, and ignoring everybody else?

People living in ordinary society will say that spirituality is only for the saints, and those who live in a monastic order will say that ordinary people cannot truly practise truth, non-violence, compassion, kindness, love and spirituality while trapped in the world of sins. This is a dichotomy. Gandhi said, "We have to practise spirituality in everyday life, in the world; and spirituality should be available and accessible to everybody. A businessperson can be spiritual, a politician can be spiritual, a farmer can be spiritual, a househusband and a housewife can be spiritual; everybody can be spiritual, and therefore spirituality belongs to everybody, not only to monks."

When I read this, my hair stood on end. I said, "I am running away from the world – I thought the world was a trap, and I needed to be free from it in order to practise spirituality." But Gandhi was saying that you can practise spirituality in everyday life, and engage with the world. That was unsettling and disturbing. I was so unsettled that I could not sleep that night – I could not think about anything else; Gandhi's words kept going round and round in my head. I felt that he was right. Spirituality should permeate throughout life and society as the air permeates throughout the whole universe. And so after a few weeks I left the monastery and became a Gandhian pilgrim.

Chapter Six

PILGRIM'S SOUL

How many loved your moments of glad grace,
And loved your beauty, with love false or true,
But one man loved the pilgrim's soul in you,
And loved the sorrows of your changing face.

W. B. Yeats, *When You are Old*

You have known great pilgrims, like Vinoba and your mother. Who else is a pilgrim who inspires you?

There are many great pilgrims whom I look up to. The Dalai Lama, Nelson Mandela, Mother Teresa – to mention just a few well-known ones. But one particular woman who stands out in my mind was simply known as 'Peace Pilgrim'. I never met her, but wherever I went in the United States, in various travels, people kept telling me again and again about this light-footed wanderer. This woman walked all around America with a message of peace. She was not *preaching* peace, she *was* peace. She carried no money, no sleeping bag, no books, no cameras, not even a note-pad. People told me that the only possession she had was a toothbrush; the greatest possession she had was that of trust. When I talk about my pilgrimages, people often ask me, "Can a woman make such a pilgrimage, without money and on foot?" I find such questions strange, and I tell people about the example of Peace Pilgrim.

Here was a woman travelling in a culture full of men who look at a woman on her own, with no money and no protection, as easy sexual prey. People advised her, "Don't do it, don't go alone, don't go without money and don't go walking. You are a woman and you are vulnerable. If you insist, then take a knife, or take a gun – don't take the risk." She would reply, "No, I'm taking nothing, I'm only taking my toothbrush and a tunic that says 'Peace Pilgrim'. I've given up my old name; I'm walking for peace, and my new identity is 'Peace Pilgrim'."

I have been told a story that one day she was walking through an incredible snowstorm which had came upon her very suddenly. Her destination was still some way off, and the place she was coming from was far behind. Darkness was falling and it would soon be night. She could not carry on walking in this snowstorm in the dark evening. It was really getting dangerous, and she needed to take shelter somewhere. Suddenly she saw a car parked in a lay-by, behind a snow drift. Inside it she found a man who was also stuck in the storm and could not carry on driving. Two souls stuck in the snow. She realised that she had to go over and ask this man to let her sleep in his car, or she would die in the snow. Sometimes pilgrims have to make such decisions for survival. She went to the car, and the man offered her shelter, "Of course you can stay in my car tonight." She passed a peaceful night in the car. However, the next morning the man confessed to her that when he let her into his car, he had thought of taking advantage of her. "But the moment you got into the car and I felt your trust towards me, I realised that I couldn't do anything to harm you, and when I saw the 'Peace Pilgrim' words on your tunic, I was stunned to see a woman devoting her life to peace. I was filled with admiration. Please tell me if I can do anything to help."

Although Peace Pilgrim is not as famous as some others I have mentioned, for me she is a profound example of a true pilgrim.

The story of Peace Pilgrim is a spiritual story. The stories of your mother, of Vinoba and Gandhi are also spiritual stories. It seems your emphasis is on the spiritual. Would you say that our crisis about which we have talked is more of a spiritual crisis than a political, environmental or social crisis? Would you call your philosophy and your approach spiritualism?

No, I would not. That again leads us into a one-dimensional thinking. You have added 'ism' to the spiritual. The moment that 'ism' is added to any word, that philosophy becomes one-dimensional. The moment you make anything into an 'ism' it becomes exclusive, dogmatic and obsessive. I would like no 'isms' whatsoever. Individualism, Communalism, Communism, Socialism, Capitalism, Buddhism, Hinduism; any 'ism' is problematic. I would like all 'isms' to become 'wasms'; let there be no more 'isms'.

A philosophy free of 'ism' accommodates all philosophies. There is no single truth, there is no single answer, there is no single philosophy which can answer all questions. Every question is a particular question, and needs a particular answer. Every situation is a particular situation, and needs a particular response. Every text has to be understood within a particular context. As a pilgrim I see life as impermanent, provisional, uncertain and emergent. The moment we commit ourselves to an 'ism' we are sacrificing spontaneity. We are blocking a potential solution which could emerge. Every moment is pregnant with umpteen possibilities, surprises and revelations. If we become wedded to an 'ism', even if it is 'spiritualism', we are still in danger of closing ourselves off from the emergence of new possibilities. Let us embrace the spiritual without the 'ism'. Also, let us embrace matter without the 'ism'. Let us embrace the environment without the 'ism'. Let us embrace the feminine without the 'ism'.

Spiritualism has another problem, it is associated with the idea of spirits coming back; as if the human spirit is here, then when we die it goes somewhere, then it comes back. That's a very reductionist understanding of the spirit. The human spirit is always present, like space is always present. You don't have to bring space from somewhere. For example, a house is built within space, but if you take the walls away, the space will remain. So the human spirit always remains everywhere, and the body embodies the spirit. When one body is gone, a new entity embodies the spirit. In the manner of speaking we are differentiating between body and spirit; it is only for the convenience of language. When we transcend language, in that sphere body and spirit are the same, and therefore there is no need for either spiritualism or materialism.

But there are some people who connect with departed spirits, and communicate with them.

That is because spirits never disappear. They are always present. And those who have the ability to connect with the spirits are able to communicate with them. It is a bit like a television aerial, which can capture the pictures which our naked eyes cannot capture. Why is it that we can see pictures on a television screen and not on an ordinary wall? It is because the television set has the right components configured in a particular way such that it is capable of capturing the pictures. In a similar way there are some human beings whose particular configuration enables them to communicate with spirits.

Just as some people, like Mozart, have a special facility to imagine and hear in their heads an entire opera and write it down, or Shakespeare could visualise King Lear, others can communicate with unseen spirits. We could also ask the question: if Mozart or Shakespeare had such special abilities, why doesn't every human being have them? It is because while we all share some common qualities, yet each one of us is endowed with some unique qualities, particular ways of seeing and experiencing the world. Just as certain discs can play music, while others show films, some of us can communicate with the living, and others with the dead. Shakespeare is no less in touch with the spirit of King Henry IV than a medium might be in touch with the King's ghost. And the one who can communicate with the ghost of King Henry may not be able to write the play, and the one who can write the play may not be able to communicate with the ghost. They are simply different ways of getting in touch with the non-physical and non-local, at the level of consciousness and imagination.

Through our strong, rational conditioning, we have come to think that if something is not logical, mathematical, empirical, then it does not exist. In this way of thinking we are narrowing down the enormous possibilities which exist in human consciousness. Due to the way our minds are moulded we have discarded astrology, telepathy, premonitions and the power of prayer. But recently even medical doctors have been able to experiment with non-local treatment and distant healing. An American doctor, Larry Dossey, has spent many years doing research on distant healing, and has evidence of it working.

In my own life I had the experience of being healed. Once I developed ringworm on the back of my hand. For months I tried all kinds of ointments, given to me by my doctor, but nothing worked. One day I heard from a friend that there was a woman healer in my village. Somewhat sceptical but in a state of desperation, I went along. The woman looked at my ringworm, silently mouthed some charm for a few seconds and said, "It will go away." And so it did: within 24 hours the ringworm completely disappeared and has never come back. No one can explain to me how or why this happened.

I myself have never experienced the presence of ghosts or spirits, but I have met people who have, and I have no reason to doubt them. Why would they lie or pretend? So I take it in the same way as I would say that I am not capable of composing *The Magic Flute*, but it is evident that Mozart could do it. Just because I cannot do something does not mean somebody else cannot do it. Human potential and human possibilities have no limits, and I am open to surprises, to incredible events and inexplicable miracles.

We are all connected with our ancestors, with the departed. Some of us are able to experience that connection implicitly and others explicitly.

You want us to be all-inclusive – science, spirituality, empiricism, intuition – everything has a place in your worldview. But mainstream society is far from that way of thinking. Are you optimistic that things will change, and that your holistic and inclusive worldview will prevail?

Yes, I am an optimist, but my optimism is a mixture of hope and action. There is no point in dwelling in pessimism. Pessimism is disempowering. If you say that things will never change, and there's nothing we can do, then it's a recipe for inaction and hopelessness, a recipe for disempowerment. I want to participate in the co-evolutionary process. In order to participate, I trust in the process of the Universe. The Universe is moving in its own evolutionary cycle. In that evolutionary cycle we will evolve. Nothing is permanent; change is inherent to existence. This idea of evolution that I am talking about is more than the Darwinian idea of evolution through natural selection. I am talking about evolution at the level of consciousness. I wish to participate in a positive way, rather than create a blockage. Pessimism creates blockages. Pessimism is an obstacle to evolution.

Evolution is not trying to reach a destination, it does not have a final point. It is not that one day we reach a state where we stop evolving. It is a continuous process. Evolution also does not mean getting better or worse – it is a transformative process. Take the example of a camera: 20 or 30 years ago people made fantastic films with old types of camera. Today we use digital cameras. It is not to say that the old cameras are bad, and the digital cameras are good, they are just different. From a certain point of view, the old cameras might be considered better, but from another point of view, digital cameras could be considered better. Nevertheless, the camera has evolved. The way we make films has been totally transformed. So evolution and transformation are twins; they go hand in hand.

The evolutionary process is bound to transform the way we live now. Although there will never be an omega point, I believe that we are evolving towards a state of universal consciousness where we will realise that we are all connected. This is the new mind, a universal mind, a divine mind, towards which we are evolving. This is spiritual evolution going hand in hand with biological evolution. The scientist Charles Darwin and the Indian mystic Sri Aurobindo meet at this point. I am very excited by such a possibility. Isn't it wonderful to have science and mysticism converging? How could one be a pessimist at this juncture? This evolution is the evolution of love, of compassion, of connectivity. If we evolve spiritually, biologically, scientifically and technologically all together, then that is a profound evolution.

Pilgrimage facilitates evolution. Biological evolution happens because our bodies and the life force within it are flexible, dynamic, responsive, living and ever-changing. That flexibility facilitates evolution. Being on a pilgrimage has similar qualities. A pilgrim's mind is a flexible mind, an open mind, a responsive mind, a living mind. And that flexibility of the mind facilitates the evolution of consciousness.

One cannot be a pilgrim with a static, dogmatic, or fixed mind. When I am on pilgrimage I am moving mentally as well as physically. That movement, that dynamism, aids and stimulates the evolutionary process in unexpected ways. If the mind is not a pilgrim's mind, meaning pliable, receptive and creative, then consciousness will stop evolving. That is why we all need to cultivate a pilgrim's mind, so that our consciousness can evolve and we can experience the new.

Why should the pilgrim's mind be free and fresh and flexible? Because the pilgrim is on the quest of overcoming attachment to things. Attachment brings suffering. If a pilgrim is attached to an idea, to a belief, to a truth, that is still an attachment. There is no one truth, there are truths, there is no one god, there are gods. The plurality of truths and gods can free us from the attachment to a fixed position. If problems arise from attachment to things, then attachment to truth or to ideals will not solve problems; only our freedom from attachment, from material or spiritual possessions, will lead to liberation. As Einstein said, "You cannot solve a problem with the same mindset which created the problem in the first place." That is why the pilgrim, by continuously letting go of his ideas and ideals, thoughts and theories, has the possibility to allow something entirely unanticipated and unpredictable, something completely new, to emerge.

Scientist David Bohm put these same thoughts in his book *Wholeness and the Implicate Order*. He was a prophet of evolution as a dynamic process of wholeness.

Siddhartha could evolve into Buddha consciousness and Jesus could evolve into Christ consciousness because their minds were completely fresh and free, dynamic and alert. They were not fixed in any kind of dogmatism, prejudice or belief system. Why is it that so many people who try to be religious, who seek enlightenment, remain stuck where they are? Because they are bound within an inflexible belief system, closed in an airtight box of dogmas, so naturally there is no evolution of consciousness.

This fixedness is not limited to religious or scientific circles. Even environmentalists long for 'utopias', havens where all will be well. We will all use solar energy, grow and eat organic food and live in a self-sufficient local economy; there will be a new settled, ecological world order. That is not only an impossible longing, it is also an unreal dream. A pilgrim's dream is a dream of continuous movement, change and evolving process.

All this sounds delightful, but distant. Maybe one day such evolution will happen, but right now the world seems to be falling apart all around us.

Are you looking properly at the world around you? It is not just falling apart, it is also coming together. What is falling apart is the old world, the old consciousness, old economics, old politics and old ways of doing business. Let that be so. Let that fall apart. There is a new consciousness emerging. New forms of politics are on the horizon. A few years ago, who would have thought that the mighty regime of apartheid in South Africa would come to an end? Who would have thought that, after 27 years in jail, Nelson Mandela (who had been condemned as a terrorist) would be freed and would become president of the new South Africa? Who would have thought that whites and blacks would meet and go through the process of truth and reconciliation? But all that happened in front of our own eyes. How could you be pessimistic?

In 1964 I was in the United States. One day I went to a restaurant for a cup of tea with a white friend in the city of Albany, Georgia. I was thrown out of that restaurant at gunpoint because it was a 'whites only' restaurant. Forty-four years later we have Barack Obama as the president of the USA. When he was born in 1961, black people did not have the right to vote. What an evolution, what a transformation! Are you still a pessimist? It is wonderful that for the first time a black family is in the White House, although Barack Obama himself is neither completely black nor white; he is both. So he can transcend and unite the two.

There may be some people who are trying to cling to the old world, but I tell you: the old world is going, going and will be gone. I can see your point – that the world seems to be falling apart – but which world? The world of globalisation, the world of banking, hedge funds, living on credit and going into debt; the world of self-interested politics, celebrity art, commercial entertainment, consumerism, superpower hegemony – all that is falling apart. But who wants to save it? The new world of organic farming, farmers' markets, renewable energy, decentralised politics, local economy and transition towns is emerging. All this may seem small and insignificant to you, but in their time how small and insignificant were the movements led by Martin Luther King and Nelson Mandela? Nevertheless, the once-powerful philosophy of apartheid and racial discrimination has lost its grip and is disappearing. I believe that the old economy and the old politics will meet the same fate. So let us have the audacity of hope, as Obama has said.

Moreover, optimism has nothing to do with the outcome, the achievements or the results. Optimism is built upon the foundation of right vision, right intention and right action. We must act according to our conscience: we must do what is the right thing to do, we must be who we want to be, and leave the results in the hands of the universe, or in the hands of god, if you like. We cannot determine the date and time of transformation. We cannot choose the pace of evolution. We can only be a part of the process and go with the flow, and the flow is moving in the direction of the unity of the world, in which people of all nations can co-operate. And humankind can live in harmony with the natural world. This very vision makes me hopeful, grateful, and an activist.

It sounds very simple. This is a great vision, and at times I see it clearly, then at other times I lose faith and feel too weak to embrace such a vision.

To be a pilgrim is to be on a path of adventure, to move out of our old comfort zones of certainty and to learn to be comfortable with uncertainty, with surprises and with the unpredictable. We have to let go of our prejudices and preconditioning, to make strides towards the unknown. It is a natural human condition to be afraid of the unknown. But the holy grail is not a tourist destination! There are no guidebooks, there are no road-maps, you cannot book your accommodation in advance!

When we consciously become pilgrims, our journey becomes a hero's journey. The mythologist Joseph Campbell talked about this journey. Heroes are those who are prepared to take their lives in their hands. They are not afraid of risks. They are not self-centred, because they are totally and unreservedly dedicated to their quest. The Buddha was a hero of this kind. He left behind his princely palace, his wife and child, his wealth and comfort, his servants and courtiers. He moved out of his comfort zone, seeking the end of human suffering. He did not contemplate for a moment the impossibility of the task. The innocence of his mind was such that he was prepared to go through any difficulties, any problems, any obstacles, to fulfil his quest.

Please do not think that it was only possible for Buddha to do this. We all have similar potential and the possibility to undertake our own quest. We need not follow the same quest as the Buddha; if we did there would be no evolution of consciousness. But if we pursue our natural calling, our own pilgrimage, our journey will turn into a hero's journey. But so often, due to family pressures, limited education and lack of self-esteem, we do not even know our deepest passions, and we are always discouraged from following our hearts. The potential for us to go on a hero's journey is blocked.

At the beginning of the journey you feel weak because you have been conditioned to be cautious. You have been pressured to play safe. You have been encouraged to walk on the well-trodden path; get a degree, get married, get a house, get a job, get insurance, get a pension, have security, look to your self-interest. These are recipes to divert you away from the hero's journey. When I started my pilgrimage for peace, and set off on my walk around the world, I too felt weak, I too was discouraged, but I managed to overcome my weakness through devotion to my ideal: the quest for peace and unity in the world, which moved me beyond my fears and gave me strength in my weak moments.

We all hunger for spiritual renewal. In our unconscious we all wish to become pilgrims, but we fear that being a pilgrim is too difficult. I feared it myself. But then I realised that there was nothing that I needed to become a pilgrim. I only needed to know that I was already a pilgrim, I needed to recognise my pilgrim quality, start to live as a pilgrim, act as a pilgrim, walk as a pilgrim, talk as a pilgrim, think as a pilgrim. Every act has to be transformed into the act of a pilgrim. A pilgrim is unburdened, always travels light. This is not only in terms of what one has in one's rucksack: it was easy to reduce the quantity of possessions in my rucksack, but it was very difficult to reduce the quantity of possessions in my head. My head was burdened with the baggage of fear, anxiety, doubt and worry – these were the heaviest pieces of luggage. I struggled to shed this baggage and lighten the burden. When I was able to travel light, without fear or anxiety, I felt easy. When I did that I became a pilgrim. I came to a state where nothing was mine. Neither material possessions nor mental possessions. As John O'Donohue said:

> I would like to live
> Like a river flows
> Carried by the surprise,
> Of its own unfolding.

There is nothing so special about being a pilgrim and going on a pilgrimage. The rivers are constantly on pilgrimage, always moving into unknown territory. No obstacle stops them, for they always find their way to move on. The wind is always on pilgrimage, following no particular route; one day it goes from south to north, another day from east to west, ever changeable and playful. Birds are always on a pilgrimage, swooping through the air, resting in their nests or on a branch, migrating thousands of miles from north to south, and from south to north again. Why can I not be the same? Why can I not be like water, wind or birds? Of course I can, when I have no feeling of acquisition or possession.

Being on a pilgrimage does not necessarily mean travelling from one place to another; that is just one way. The trees are on pilgrimage, so are the mountains, they are in movement although they are not on the move. They are evolving, growing, and being in harmony with the rest of nature. Most of all, the Earth itself is on a pilgrimage, continuously moving around the sun, and we are all part of that pilgrimage. But that does not mean that the sun itself is not on pilgrimage. It is on the pilgrimage of enlightenment. In essence I realised that being a pilgrim is a state of mind, a state of consciousness, a state of fearlessness.

What surprised me was that when I let go of my fears of the unknown, I discovered that all those fears were actually unfounded: those dangers and problems existed only in my mind. When I was on my peace pilgrimage, love and enthusiasm were poured over me by people who knew nothing of me. They offered me hospitality, saying, "Where are the pilgrims? We long to welcome them but they hardly ever come!"

You have been the editor of *Resurgence* magazine for the past 35 years. Through the pages of this publication you have been informing and inspiring readers. Wholeness, integrity, gratitude and love are at the heart of *Resurgence*. These qualities flow from the magazine's pages.

Initially my wife June and I undertook the editorship of *Resurgence* for a short time, as we wanted to work with the Gandhian movement in India. Then I met E. F. Schumacher, the author of *Small is Beautiful*, who persuaded us to stay in the UK and continue to edit the magazine. When I said to him that I wish to go back to India and work with the Gandhian movement he said, "There are many Gandhians in India, Satish; we need one in England!" That was a very compelling invitation, so June and I decided to stay. At that time we were living in London. Although we enjoyed the editorship, meeting authors and illustrators, communicating with readers and subscribers, living in London proved to be hard. The life of the city was stressful: too much time spent commuting, too many people, too many shops, too many streets, too many cars, too much noise; not enough time, not enough friendship, no gardening – exactly the opposite of the values and vision of *Resurgence*.

After a few years the opportunity arose to move out of London, and eventually to come and live in Devon. We found a house in the country where we could live a simple life, grow our own food, go for walks, and work where we lived so that we didn't have to commute. The *Resurgence* office is across the yard, so I can work from home. In 1973 when we took on the editorship, we were printing 500 copies of the magazine, now we are printing 15,000.

The success of *Resurgence* is based on trust, patience, commitment and dedication. Publishing a magazine with integrity and idealism is not easy: most magazines finance themselves through advertising, but *Resurgence* is not a commercial venture and we wouldn't accept any unethical, unecological advertising. If we were to charge the real cost of each issue, we would price ourselves out of the market. So the only way we can sustain *Resurgence* is through philanthropic grants, donations and the goodwill of our supporters. About 80% of our income is from subscriptions and about 20% is from donations.

Of course we have gone through difficulties, through frugal times and hardship. At times it was doubtful that the magazine would survive. But we kept our faith, commitment and enthusiasm. When you have determination and you are open to the gifts of the universe, then gifts do come along! Sometimes the gifts come and pass by, and we don't notice them. So the art is to keep your heart open, your mind open, your doors open. Whenever any possibility or opportunity arrived I welcomed it with gratitude. This is how we have managed to keep *Resurgence* going and flourishing for the past 35 years. Now *Resurgence* is a registered charitable trust, so I think its future is good.

You seem to be completely absorbed in editing *Resurgence*, yet while doing this you managed to go on pilgrimages.

Yes, at age 50 I walked around the sacred sites of Britain, circumambulating the British Isles, a journey which lasted four months. When I was 60 I went around holy Mount Kailash, walking over the 18,000-foot-high pass. Those were explicit pilgrimages, which I have described in detail in my autobiography *No Destination* and in *You Are, Therefore I Am*, which is a collection of memoirs and encounters with people I met during my pilgrimages.

These journeys bring me the realisation of how little I need to sustain myself. When I am at home surrounded by objects of comfort and convenience I begin to think that without them I cannot survive, but I could walk around Britain for four months with one change of clothes and no money – how did I do it? Being on that journey gave me a sense of sufficiency and completeness without the need for and dependence on umpteen possessions. With that realisation, even when I am at home I can live lightly and in a detached manner.

Being away from your home, being in nature and in the wild have been a perennial source of liberation. Christian pilgrims became 'desert fathers' and lived on little, yet found profound inner riches. Jesus Christ himself went into the desert and discovered the enchantment of the spirit within. Ever since that time Christians from all over Europe have created a network of pilgrim routes to holy places – going through the quiet, isolated and peaceful landscapes of the wild. Even St Francis of Assisi joined pilgrims on one of these routes which led to Santiago de Compostela. The pilgrim's spirit combined with an outer journey is like truth combined with beauty; and beauty becomes even more beautiful when it is also truthful, as Shakespeare wrote:

O how much more doth beauty beauteous seem
By that sweet ornament which Truth doth give!

When my outer journey and my inner journey are in harmony and integrated, then I smell the pilgrim spirit in my consciousness. This pilgrim spirit is like the fragrance of the rose. The perfume makes the rose rosier; the pilgrim's spirit makes the journey sacred. As Shakespeare continued:

> *The rose looks fair, but fairer we it deem*
> *For that sweet odour which doth in it live.*

Being on a journey has parallels to the Shakespearean metaphor:

> *All the world's a stage*
> *And all the men and women merely players:*
> *They have their exits and their entrances;*
> *And one man in his time plays many parts.*

In this metaphor there is no fixed, static state of being: it's all change, all movement, all coming and going. There is no attachment to a particular role; we all know that it is only a play – what Hindus call *Lila*. So there is no need to get bogged down, no need to cling to a particular role, for everything is a passing phase.

Editing *Resurgence* is also a pilgrimage of its own kind. Through *Resurgence* I am able to relate, to connect, to serve, to evolve, and to celebrate without attachment. It is a journey into wholeness.

I have come to enjoy every action in itself; for every action is a complete action. A seed is a complete seed, a tree is a complete tree, a bud is a complete bud. The bud does not need to become a flower to complete itself, for it is already complete; when it is a flower, it is also complete; and when the flower turns into fruit, that fruit is also complete. And then of course there is that complete seed again, deep within the fruit. This sense of completeness, wholeness, is always with me. All stages of completeness are complete in themselves, and yet, completely related to the previous and forthcoming stages. The seed is related to the tree, the bud is related to the flower, the fruit is related to the seed; thus there is a completeness, a continuum and a relatedness simultaneously.

Nothing is incomplete. Cooking is not incomplete, even though eating has not yet begun. Cooking is not to achieve the result of cooking. Cooking itself is a sacred act. Whether eating or not eating, I can still enjoy the act of cooking. Similarly, eating is not incomplete, even though digestion and nourishment have not yet begun. I can still enjoy the pleasure of eating. Washing-up is not incomplete, even though we do not yet need the pots to cook again. I can enjoy the process of washing-up for its own sake.

There is a Sanskrit verse about this:

Poornamadah
Poornamidum
Poornat poornamudachayte
Poornasya poornamadaya
Poornamevavshisyate

This is complete,
That is complete,
What comes out of complete is also complete;
Having taken the complete out of the complete,
What remains is complete.

There is nothing other than completeness. Every word is complete, every syllable is complete, every sentence is complete, every page is complete, every book is complete, every library is complete, everything is complete.

These words come from the Upanishads. Everything is complete in itself, and therefore we pilgrims do not hanker for results, for the fruit, for the achievement of our action. When we are detached from the fruit of our action and are fully present in our action, then we are present in the here and now. Every action happens only in the here and now. Thus action is its own fulfilment.

This is the state of the pilgrim's mind: the pilgrim is related to everything but is owner of nothing, possesses nothing. This is because when I own something I am incomplete without it, and it is incomplete without me. But if everything is complete in itself, finding meaning in its relatedness, then everything has its own identity and its own integrity. A pilgrim acts in a detached manner without being the owner of the action: I am not the doer, for actions are happening through me. Every action has its integrity, as I have my integrity. It is like a dance, a happening, complete in itself. The dancer is not in control of the dance, he or she is the vehicle of the dance, and the dance is transforming the dancer while the dancer is forming the dance.

You can make an effort to dance well, but a great dance just happens. We can only practise, we can only act; practice is our prerogative, but the results are beyond our control. So the Bhagavad Gita teaches us: "Neither give up the practice and the action, nor bind yourself with the desires for the results and the fruits of your action." Using modern terminology, we can say that the results are an 'emergent property'.

When I speak to you, words are emerging. I do not possess the words, I do not possess my voice, or my thoughts. If you put my brain under a microscope, you will not find any thoughts there. My brain is only processing thoughts, as a television screen is processing pictures which are not inside the set; my brain is processing words which are coming from the universe, and going back into the universe. I let the noble thoughts come to me from all corners of the universe, as the Vedas have proclaimed.

And thus ever, by day and night, under the sun and under the stars, climbing the dusty hills and toiling along the weary planes, journeying by land and journeying by sea, coming and going so strangely, to meet and to act and react on one another, move all we restless travellers through the pilgrimage of life.

Charles Dickens, *Little Dorrit*

NO DESTINATION
An autobiography

"One of the few life-changing books I have ever read. I wish everyone would read it." –Thomas Moore, author of *Care of the Soul*

When he was only nine years old, Satish Kumar renounced the world and joined the wandering brotherhood of Jain monks. Dissuaded from this path by an inner voice at the age of eighteen, he became a campaigner for land reform, working to turn Gandhi's vision of a renewed India into reality. Fired by the example of Bertrand Russell, he undertook an 8,000-mile peace pilgrimage, walking from India to America without any money, through mountains, deserts, storms and snow. It was an adventure during which he was thrown into jail in France, faced a loaded gun in America – and delivered packets of 'peace tea' to the leaders of the four nuclear powers.

In 1973 he settled in England, taking on the editorship of *Resurgence* magazine, and becoming the guiding light behind a number of ecological, spiritual and educational ventures. Following Indian tradition, in his fiftieth year he undertook another pilgrimage: again without any money, he walked to the holy places of Britain – Glastonbury Lindisfarne and Iona.

Written with a penetrating simplicity, *No Destination* is an exhilarating account of an extraordinary life.

Green Books 320pp 216 x 138mm
ISBN 978 1 870098 89 2 £9.95 paperback
www.greenbooks.co.uk

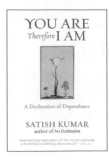

YOU ARE, THEREFORE I AM
A Declaration of Dependence

"The life of this vigorous, wise, compassionate and humble man is an example to all of us about how to make the most of our gifts and create our own opportunities to serve humanity's future."
– Hazel Henderson, author of *Creating Alternative Futures*

"Satish Kumar is, for me, the sage of the deep ecology movement." – Fritjof Capra, author of *The Web of Life*

Tracing his own spiritual journey, Satish Kumar considers the sources of inspiration which formed his understanding of the world as a network of multiple and diverse relationships. The book is in four parts. The first describes his memories of conversations with his mother, his teacher and his guru, all of whom were deeply religious. The second part recounts his discussions with the Indian sage Vinoba Bhave, J. Krishnamurti, Bertrand Russell, Martin Luther King and E. F. Schumacher. These five great activists and thinkers inspired him to engage with social, ecological and political issues. In the third part Satish narrates his travels in India, which have continued to nourish his mind and reconnect him with his roots. The fourth part brings together his worldview, which is based in relationships and the connections between all things, encapsulated in a fundamental Sanskrit dictum '*So Hum*', well-known in India but not in the West, which can be translated as 'You are, therefore I am'.

Green Books 192pp 234 x 156mm
ISBN 978 1 1903998 18 2 £9.95 paperback
www.greenbooks.co.uk

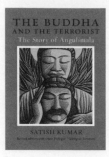

THE BUDDHA AND THE TERRORIST

The Story of Angulimala

"It has a lucid clarity and directness that speaks pointedly and movingly to our times. It should touch every heart that meets it."
– Pico Iyer, author of *The Global Soul*

Once upon a time in northern India, there lived a violent and fearsome outcaste called Angulimala ('necklace of fingers'). He terrorised towns and villages in order to try to gain control of the state, murdering people and adding their fingers to his gruesome necklace.

The Buddha set out to meet Angulimala, and with the power of love and compassion he persuaded him to renounce violence and take responsibility for his past actions. Thus Angulimala was transformed. *The Buddha & the Terrorist* brings a message for our time about the importance of looking for the root causes of violence, and of finding peaceful means to end terror.

Green Books 96pp 174 x 123mm
ISBN 978 1 903998 63 2 £4.95 paperback
www.greenbooks.co.uk

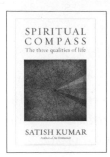

SPIRITUAL COMPASS
The Three Qualities of Life

"Satish Kumar's life is an admirable example of simplicity, compassion and care, and this shines through on every page of this delightful, yet profound, little book."
– Peter Russell, author of *Waking Up in Time*

"*Spiritual Compass* offers clear and joyful evidence of the bridge that can and must be built between the great spiritual teachings of the East and the onrushing, bedeviled life of our contemporary world. May there come many others who join Satish Kumar in this essential work!"
– Jacob Needleman, author of *Why Can't We Be Good*

Spirituality needs to be a part of our ordinary, everyday existence: it needs to be implicitly present in business, politics, farming, cooking – and in our relationships. In *Spiritual Compass*, Satish Kumar draws on the Indian Ayurvedic tradition, which characterises the mind as having three *gunas*, or primary qualities: *sattva* (characterised by calmness, clarity and purity), *rajas* (energy and passion) and *tamas* (dullness and ignorance). The Ayurvedic aim is to live a life that is simple and close to nature (sattvic), to reduce rajasic tendencies, and to avoid tamasic ones. When we see ourselves in the light of the three gunas, they can help us to recover the art of living, and lead us towards a peaceful and contented existence.

Green Books 144pp 222 x 141mm
ISBN 978 1 1903998 89 2 £9.95 hardback
www.greenbooks.co.uk

Resurgence

Satish Kumar is Editor of *Resurgence* magazine, described in *The Guardian* as "the spiritual and artistic flagship of the green movement". If you would like a sample copy of a recent issue, please contact:

Jeanette Gill, Rocksea Farmhouse,
St. Mabyn, Bodmin, Cornwall PL30 3BR
Telephone 01208 841824 Fax 01208 841256
www.resurgence.org

He is also a Visiting Fellow at Schumacher College, an international centre for ecological studies. For the latest course programme, please contact:

The Administrator, Schumacher College,
The Old Postern, Dartington, Totnes, Devon TQ9 6EA
Telephone 01803 865934 Fax 01803 866899
www.schumachercollege.org.uk

EARTH PILGRIM DVD

"You'll probably have seen similar sights in documentaries but you'll never have felt their impact so acutely." – *Daily Mail* Preview

"Some truly spectacular cinematography" – Morwenna Ferrier, *The Observer*

The *Earth Pilgrim* film takes viewers on a journey through the seasons of Dartmoor and explores our profound relationship with the natural world. It is an Eastern view of the West, seen through the eyes of Jain monk, world-renown conservationist and pacifist, Satish Kumar. This film is a 'meditation on the moor', that portrays an engrossing picture of Satish Kumar's philosophy and reverence for the living Earth. According to a *BBC Wildlife Magazine* review, "Our leaders should make his insightfulness an integral part of their manifestos. It would be a better world if Bush applied some of Kumar's principles – and meant them."

Finalist: Cinematography, Wildscreen Film Festival 2008

Available through www.resurgence.org